BUILD
A KICKA$$
ONLINE COMMUNITY

Practical Engagement Tactics

BY DR. EVE KEDAR

Foreword by renowned community builder Eva Forde

Published by: GWN Publishing
www.GWNPublishing.com

Cover Design: Kristina Conatser

ISBN: 978-1-965971-11-6

DEDICATION

To Kibbutz Alonim and my Maayan classmates, who planted the first seeds of community in my heart. Your embrace taught me that belonging is both a birthright and a practice, and that true community requires both roots and wings. Those early lessons continue to nourish everything I create today.

To Loretta J. Ross, whose profound wisdom about "calling in" rather than "calling out" has forever changed how we can approach building inclusive, transformative communities. Though we've never met, your teachings light the way toward more compassionate and effective community building.

To the leaders and participants of online communities who show up daily to create spaces of belonging, growth, and transformation. Your dedication to building meaningful connections in our digital world inspires this work. I especially appreciate all those who answered my interview questions with generous thoughtfulness and care.

And to all the kickass people who understand that true community isn't just about gathering, it's about growing together, supporting each other, and creating spaces where everyone can thrive.

May this book help create more spaces where people feel seen, heard, and valued.

"A community is the single most powerful way to navigate a highly dynamic, rapidly changing world."

—Gina Bianchini, founder of Mighty Networks

TABLE OF CONTENTS

FOREWORD

by Eva Forde

When Eve Kedar asked me to write the foreword for "Build a Kickass Online Community," I was both honored and humbled. As someone who has experienced both the triumphs and challenges of community building firsthand, I understand the transformative power of creating spaces where people truly connect.

My journey with community building has been a winding one. As a community leader in Seth Godin's Carbon Almanac project, I had the privilege of helping mobilize and coordinate 300 people from forty-one countries. My role involved welcoming newcomers, connecting people based on their skills and interests, and creating community-wide systems that kept folks aligned and moving forward. Through intentional community leadership, we accomplished the seemingly impossible: In just 120 days, we produced a 97,000-word book, complete with illustrations, a podcast network, a LinkedIn course, a comprehensive resource collection, an educator's guide, a children's edition, a daily newsletter, and an online visual knowledge base—all for free. The experience showed me in real time the extraordinary potential of well-structured communities with a clear purpose and intentional culture.

But I've also experienced failure. When I founded the Rich Social Workers Facebook group, I naively believed that "if you build it, they will come" was a complete strategy. I simply followed Facebook's basic setup guidelines, invited some connections, and expected magic to happen. What I discovered instead was that thriving communities don't create themselves—they require intention, structure, and continuous nurturing.

This is precisely why Eve's book couldn't have arrived at a better moment. Now as my team and I prepare to launch Ripple, a community for our Social Work Wealth Conference attendees, we're determined to create something truly meaningful. Eve's practical playbook offers exactly what practitioners like us need: not just theory but actionable tactics for fostering genuine engagement, growth, and connection.

What strikes me most about Eve's approach is her understanding that successful communities aren't about member counts or platform features—they're about creating spaces where people feel seen, heard, and empowered to grow. As she eloquently puts it, communities are "engines of transformation" built on belonging, support, and growth.

Whether you're a seasoned community builder looking to level up your skills, a creator seeking to unite your audience, or a business leader aiming to build something more meaningful than just another Facebook group, this book offers a road map grounded in both psychology and practicality.

In a world where digital connections often feel shallow and transactional, Eve reminds us that true community—the kind that changes lives and creates lasting transformation—is both an art and a science. This book masterfully addresses both dimensions, offering insights into the human need for belonging alongside tactical guidance on platform selection, engagement strategies, and sustainable growth.

As you embark on your community-building journey, know that you're not just creating another online space—you're creating the possibility for genuine human connection in a world that desperately needs it. Eve's playbook will be your trusted guide every step of the way.

Here's to building something truly kickass!

Eva Forde

Founder, Social Work Wealth Conference
impact@richsocialworker.com
richsocialworker.com

ACKNOWLEDGMENTS

This book would not have been possible without the generous contributions of many individuals who shared their time, expertise, and experiences.

I am deeply grateful to everyone who participated in interviews and provided insights that shaped this work: Your willingness to share your community-building journeys brought depth and authenticity to these pages. I'm especially grateful to the many generous and thoughtful people who are part of Purple Space.

Special thanks to those who reviewed early drafts and offered invaluable feedback. Your thoughtful comments helped refine and strengthen the ideas presented here.

I'm indebted to the entire team at GWN Publishing who believed in this project and helped bring it to life.

The journey of writing this book was supported by many friends and colleagues who offered encouragement, listened to my ideas, and cheered me on through challenges: You are loved and appreciated.

And finally, my heartfelt appreciation goes to the readers and community builders who will take these ideas forward in ways I cannot yet imagine. Your work continues to inspire and motivate me.

INTRODUCTION

A Playbook to Build On

We live in a world that is both constantly connected and increasingly disconnected, where technology has multiplied our touchpoints while decreasing our engagement with people who can nourish and uplift our souls.

Since the Web was born, its denizens have felt the elemental urge to form meaningful connections online with groups of other humans, early on in simple chat rooms and later in full-blown communities. Social commentator Harold Rheingold, author of The Virtual Community, explains the phenomenon this way: "Virtual communities are social aggregations that emerge from the net when enough people carry on those public discussions long enough, with sufficient human feeling, to form webs of personal relationships in cyberspace."

Right now, across the digital landscape, people are finding meaningful connections in the most incredible ways. We're gathering in Brandon Burchard's Growth Day community to level up members' personal development. We're diving deep into artificial intelligence discussions in Nicole Russell's I Heart AI community. We are building businesses, sharing dreams, and supporting each other in ways that would have seemed impossible just a few years ago.

Seth Godin, an American author, entrepreneur, educator, connector, and marketing pioneer is the founder of the Purple Space community (currently home to about a thousand global members), which he built on Discourse, a respected open-source software platform for community building. He is a role model for builders like me, and his memorable quotations frequently find their way into the teaching of community founders. Here is one I think about often and share in this book: "The barriers to leadership have fallen. The internet has made it possible for everyone to create their own tribe. Embrace the tribe. **Find your people.**"

That is, in fact, what this book is about; helping you create that space where your people can find each other, grow together, and build something remarkable within a like-minded tribe. Whether you're dreaming of a vibrant community around shared interests, a professional network that delivers value, or a supportive space for growth and transformation, you're in exactly the right place.

Throughout this book, you'll find insights from my conversations with members across diverse communities. While many generously allowed me to share their perspectives by name, some quotes appear anonymously to honor requests for privacy. This approach reflects one of our core community-building principles—creating spaces where trust flourishes and members feel secure sharing authentically. Their willingness to contribute, whether publicly or privately, has enriched this playbook immeasurably.

WHY THIS BOOK? WHY NOW?

Here's the good news, it's not about having the fanciest platform or the biggest marketing budget. It is about creating spaces where people feel seen, heard, and empowered to grow. I've watched communities on platforms like Nas.io transform from simple discussion boards into thriving ecosystems of support and opportunity. I've seen small Discourse servers become launching pads for world-changing ideas.

The secret? It's not really about the technology. It is about understanding how to bring people together in ways that matter, how to foster connections that last, and how to build systems that scale without losing their soul.

WHO THIS BOOK IS FOR

This is your practical playbook for creating something kickass and amazing.

It's meant for:

- The creator who knows their audience needs a space to connect but isn't sure where to start.

- The business leader looking to build more than just another Facebook group.

- The passion-project initiator who wants to unite people around a shared mission.

- The community manager ready to level up their skills and impact.

- Anyone who believes in the power of bringing people together.

You don't need to be a tech wizard or a social media guru. You just need to care about creating genuine connections and be willing to learn how to do it right.

HOW TO GET THE MOST OUT OF THIS BOOK

Think of this book as your community-building journey companion. Each chapter builds on the last, providing you with practical tools, real-world examples, and actionable strategies you can start using right away.

You'll find stories from successful (and not-so-successful) communities, lessons learned the hard way so you don't have to learn them yourself, and clear steps to take your community from concept to thriving reality.

YOUR INVITATION TO COMMUNITY SUCCESS

Building a community isn't just about gathering people in one place. It's about creating spaces where magic happens. Where someone can show up feeling alone and leave feeling supported. Where ideas can spark, grow, and become reality through the power of collective wisdom and support.

Now, let's get tactical about how to use this playbook to create your community-building success story.

This isn't a book you'll just read. It's one you'll use, one you'll refer to often, and one that inspires action. Each chapter is designed to build on the last, providing you with practical tools and insights you can implement immediately. Here's how to get the most out of your journey:

CHAPTER-BY-CHAPTER GUIDE

At the end of every chapter, you'll find powerful tools to support your learning and implementation:

1. *Chapter summaries:* quick, actionable recaps of key takeaways to keep you focused and moving forward

2. *Podcast and YouTube recommendations:* these help you dive deeper into the power of community

3. *Guiding questions:* Thoughtful prompts to inspire reflection. They are intended to help you connect chapter concepts to your community goals. This isn't about rushing through—it's about making meaningful progress that lasts.

4. *FAQs:* Real answers to the most common questions and challenges you're likely to face at each stage of community building

5. *Chapter worksheets:* Detailed action plans that bring together the key strategies from each chapter, helping you build your community step-by-step

6. *Other tools:* In some chapters you will also find topic-specific exercises, recommended actions, and guidelines and templates. Some of the lengthiest guidelines and templates are in the Appendixes; they are illustrative examples, all meant to be customized and adapted to your community's unique purpose, values, and goals.

The principles in this book come alive when you put them into practice. Connect with me on LinkedIn (Eve Kedar) for an exclusive invitation to join my community, where we can dive deeper into the community-building journey together.

MAKING THIS JOURNEY YOUR OWN

Here's something important to remember: Building a community should be fun! Yes, we'll cover serious strategies and practical tools like monetizing, but this journey is also about joy and discovery. Creating and nurturing those magical aha moments when everything clicks. Stay curious, experiment freely, and don't be afraid to add your own flavor to these ideas. Some of the best community innovations come from leaders who were bold enough to try something different.

This book isn't about perfection; it's about progress and enjoying the ride. Take what resonates, experiment with the ideas, and adapt them to fit your vision. The most successful communities aren't carbon copies of others; they're authentic expressions of their leaders' and members' shared purpose, built with equal parts strategy and joy.

THE POWER OF COMMUNITY IN THE DIGITAL AGE: FINDING THE OTHERS

"People like us do things like this."

—Seth Godin

Seth Godin's simple yet profound idea in the quotation above captures the heart of every great community. Building community isn't just about gathering people in one place or racking up member counts. It's about creating meaningful connections, finding your people, and doing work that matters alongside those who will travel with you, support you, and get excited about your vision for what's possible.

In today's dynamic world, changes abound, some wonderful, some worrying. The pace of change seems to be accelerating, requiring a nimble and expansive approach. Well-built, nurtured, and developed communities can serve as buffers, providing participants with a place

Seth Godin *(credit Abby Greenawalt)*

to adapt to changes, support transformation, and engage safely at a pace that suits them. In these spaces, every individual can feel seen, heard, and empowered to grow, regardless of location. Participants can drop in, hang back, engage, and thrive, achieving transformation on their own terms. This is the true power of building an online community.

As Dr. Martin Luther King Jr. eloquently stated, "We are tied together in a single garment of destiny, caught in an inescapable network of mutuality." Communities reflect this interconnectedness and shared journey.

WHY COMMUNITY MATTERS

At their core, communities are engines of transformation on three critical pillars:

1. **Belonging:** A sense of deep connection that goes beyond likes, follows, or brief interactions

2. **Support:** A network of people celebrating wins, helping navigate challenges, and offering reminders that you're not alone

3. **Growth:** Opportunities to learn, share, and transform together, not just as individuals

Take, for example, Seth Godin's Purple Space, on the Discourse community platform. This thriving community, inspired by the idea of "finding the others," is built on shared purpose and mutual support. It's intimate, intentional, and deeply impactful. Or consider Noelle Russell's I Heart AI community on Skool, which brings people together to explore the ethical implications of AI and support each other's growth in the field. Neither started with massive audiences but clear purposes and committed groups united by common goals. Brandon Burchard's Growth Day on customized Circle.so is another great example of belonging, support and growth in action.

As humans, **we're wired to seek connection.** We crave recognition, acceptance, and shared direction. Strong communities meet these needs by creating spaces where members feel acknowledged, heard, and valued. Belonging to something greater not only lifts our spirits, the connection also boosts motivation, strengthens mental health, and helps us navigate life's ups and downs.

Noelle Russell

THE PSYCHOLOGY OF BELONGING

Why do we crave community? Psychologists Roy Baumeister and Mark Leary argue that belonging is a fundamental human need, vital for well-being. In their landmark paper, "The Need to Belong," they say that humans have an innate drive to form lasting, positive relationships. This need is so universal that we see it across all cultures.

Additionally, a sense of belonging within a community has been shown to:

- Improve feelings of self-esteem and self-worth.

- Lower rates of depression and anxiety.

- Enhance overall mental and physical health.

- Provide a buffer against stress.

- Motivate people to make positive changes.

In short, communities aren't just nice to have. Communities are essential for humans to thrive. And in an increasingly digital world, online communities play a vital role in meeting this need.

CHOOSING THE RIGHT COMMUNITY PLATFORM

If you're creating an online community, one key early decision is selecting the right platform. While there are many options, some top contenders include:

- **Circle:** Provides a sleek, white-labeled community experience with robust features like courses, events, and subgroups. Used by creators like Brendon Burchard for his Growth Day community.

- **Discourse:** Offers real-time conversations with instant updates and notifications. It features robust topic management with categories and tags, and it uses a "trust level" system that grants additional privileges to active and well-regarded members. Used by Seth Godin for his Purple Space.

- **Mighty Networks:** Offers a powerful all-in-one solution with community, courses, events, and more. Allows for building a community under your own brand. An example is BuJo U by Ryder Carroll.

- **Nas.io:** A newer player focused on connecting niche communities around shared interests and goals. Used by the UAE's largest women-only community; Indian Women Dubai, founded by Reema Mahajan.

- **Skool:** An emerging platform choice for edupreneurs and course creators looking to add community to their programs. Used by Noelle Russell's I Heart AI community.

When choosing a platform, consider these key factors:

- Alignment with your brand and goals

- Available features and customization

- Ease of use for both you and members

- Potential for growth and scalability

- Existing network of communities for cross-promotion

- Costs, including integrations, monetization, and customizations

While the platform that you consider best varies according to your specific needs and your budget, the most important thing is to get started. Many successful communities began on a simple forum or

Facebook group before migrating to a more robust solution. The key is to pick a starting point and begin building, knowing you can iterate and adjust as you grow.

BUILDING YOUR FOUNDATION

With the platform selected, it's time to lay the groundwork for a thriving community. This includes:

- Gaining clarity about your ideal members and their needs.

- Developing your community's "big purpose."

- Setting up your space for success.

- Establishing the key systems to drive engagement.

- Deciding your monetization strategy (Cost of entry? Tiered access?)

We'll dive deeper into each of these areas in Chapter 2. For now, spend some time reflecting on the prompts below to start forming your community vision.

PRACTICAL EXERCISE: MAP YOUR COMMUNITY

Grab a piece of paper or open a blank document and draw a large circle to represent your community. Inside the circle, write down the key traits of the people you want to connect with:

- What do they care about?

- What motivates them?

- What challenges are they facing?

This simple exercise will help clarify who you're inviting into your space and what they're looking for.

GUIDING QUESTIONS

1. Who are the people you're trying to connect with? What are their passions, challenges, and goals?

2. How will your community create a sense of belonging? What will make it stand out from other spaces?

3. What experiences from your own life might inspire the way you build your community?

4. Which community platform aligns best with your vision and needs right now, and why?

5. How do you want to monetize?

PODCAST AND YOUTUBE RECOMMENDATIONS

> **NOTE:** These podcasts and videos were accessible at the time of writing in March 2025. If you cannot find the exact episode, please search for the people mentioned on YouTube.

*   Episode 36, "Building community, tribalism, and the principle of 'People like us do things like this,'" featuring Seth Godin on Levels. The episode discusses Seth Godin's principles about building community and the concept of "smallest viable market." The episode was released on November 1, 2021, and features a conversation between Seth Godin and Ben Grynol, head of growth at Levels, where they discuss marketing, community building, and related topics.

- "Unleashing people magic," Gina Bianchini with Catalin Matei. https://youtu.be/9StrLuQNSh4?si=JGLDiHgJImnmQDjq

- "The power of people and practices" with Brendon Burchard from Growth Day. https://podcasts.apple.com/us/podcast/the-power-of-people-practices/id821746377?i=1000619364153

FAQS

1. **I'm not a tech expert. Do I need to be an expert to build a successful online community?**

   Absolutely not! While familiarity with online platforms is helpful, the most crucial elements are your passion for your community's purpose and your commitment to fostering genuine connections. This playbook guides you through the essential tools and strategies, focusing on the human aspects of community building rather than technical wizardry. It's about creating a space where people feel valued, regardless of tech skills.

2. **There are already so many online communities. What makes this book different?**

   This book isn't just about creating another online group. It's about building a kickass community, one that's deeply engaging, provides real value, and fosters a sense of belonging. We'll dive into practical tactics and strategies, drawing from real-world examples and the author's experience. It's about moving beyond surface-level interactions to create a thriving, supportive, and impactful community that stands out.

3. How do I know if building an online community is right for me or my business?

If you're passionate about connecting with others, sharing your expertise, or building a supportive space around a shared interest, monetizing your community, then building an online community could be a fantastic for you. This book is designed for anyone who wants to create meaningful connections, whether it's for personal growth, professional networking, or business development. We'll explore how to identify your target audience, define your community's purpose, and create a space that aligns with your goals.

CHAPTER SUMMARY

Community isn't about collecting followers, it's about creating connections and building affiliations. It's where people find belonging, support, and growth. To build something meaningful, start by defining who you're trying to reach and why it matters. Keep your focus on the people, not the numbers, and create a space where they feel seen, heard, and inspired to grow together.

CHAPTER 1 WORKSHEET

The Power of Community in the Digital Age

SECTION A: FINDING YOUR PEOPLE

Community vision mapping. Draw your ideal community (use circles, arrows, or any visual format that works for you):

- **At the center:** Write your core purpose.
- **Inner circle:** List three to five key characteristics of your ideal members,
- **Outer circle:** Write the transformation they'll experience.

Your community's why. Complete these statements:

My community exists because

_____

The problem we're solving is

_____

Our members need this because

_____

The transformation we offer is

_____

SECTION B: COMMUNITY FOUNDATION ASSESSMENT

Rate your clarity (1 to 5 for best) for each element. We will return to this as we sharpen your clarity.

Clear purpose	1	2	3	4	5
Target audience	1	2	3	4	5
Unique value proposition	1	2	3	4	5
Transformation promise	1	2	3	4	5
Community culture	1	2	3	4	5
Monetization strategy	1	2	3	4	5

SECTION C: DEVELOP AN AVATAR FOR YOUR IDEAL MEMBER.

In this section, you will describe your ideal member.

Demographics and background

Professional role: _____

Experience level: _____

Key challenges: _____

Goals and aspirations: _____

Their journey

Where they are now: _____

Where they want to be: _____

Obstacles in their way: _____

How your community helps: _____

SECTION D: SPECIFIC WAYS YOU'LL FOSTER BELONGING

_____ *(Example: weekly welcome threads)*

_____ *(Example: peer mentoring program)*

_____ *(Example: celebration rituals)*

SECTION E: AVOIDING COMMON PITFALLS.

For each potential pitfall, write your prevention strategy.

Having a combination of live events and recordings:

Keeping content fresh and engaging:

Having a clear monetization strategy, including free, such as entry-paywall and tiered-paywall options:

Actions you will take if community guidelines are ignored:

SECTION F: ACTION PLANNING.

Next steps (check when completed).

☐ Write community purpose statement.

☐ Define ideal member profile.

☐ List core community values.

☐ Draft welcome process.

☐ Plan first month of content.

☐ Pitfall avoidance strategy.

SECTION G: REFLECTION AND IMPLEMENTATION.
Answer these questions.

What makes your community unique?

_____

_____

_____

How will you measure success initially?

_____

_____

_____

What act or program is your first priority to implement?

_____

_____

_____

THIRTY-DAY QUICK-START PLAN

Week one: _____

Week two: _____

Week three: _____

Week four: _____

LOOKING AHEAD

Time to set up your community for success. Now that you've got the why of community, it's time to dive into the how. In Chapter 2, we'll cover the nuts and bolts of setting up your space, cultivating the right culture, and creating an environment where people can thrive. Let's build something amazing!

Ready to dive deeper? Find me on LinkedIn and let's make your community culture legendary.

CHAPTER 2

CLARITY OF PURPOSE: YOUR COMMUNITY'S NORTH STAR

"A community is created when people agree to uphold the same values."

—Stewart Brand, a founder of The WELL, where the online community was born.

Tony Robbins has said, "Setting goals is the first step in turning the invisible into the visible." This rings especially true when building a thriving online community. Your purpose isn't just a mission statement; it's the beacon that draws your ideal members and guides them toward a shared, transformative journey.

As Eva Forde, who generously wrote the foreword and is a member of Purple Space, noted, "You don't just state your values and operations once. You repeat them often because people forget, and new members join regularly. People need to be reminded." Think of your community's purpose as your North Star, a constant, guiding light that keeps everyone aligned and inspired, especially as your community grows.

Purpose isn't just nice to have; it's the engine that drives transformative communities. It empowers members to reach their highest potential. When you build with unwavering intention, you create a beacon that ignites change and inspires action.

UNDERSTANDING YOUR IDEAL MEMBER

The foundation of a deeper purpose lies in understanding your ideal members. What are their deepest needs, their biggest challenges, and their most cherished aspirations? When you grasp these, you can craft a vision that resonates on a profound, personal level. Here are some key member archetypes to consider:

1. *Transformation seekers:* People navigating pivotal life moments who crave support, guidance, and accountability as they step into their next chapter. They bring a desire for growth and inspire others with their personal journey.

2. *Kindred spirit:*. Individuals who share your passions, values, and worldview. They're energized by going deep into the topics that light you up. These are people you find it easier to connect with and build your network.

3. *Action takers:* Members who are ready to dive in, contribute, and make real changes. They show up consistently and inspire others with their commitment. They become known for this, and people look to them for direction.

4. *Thought leaders:* Experts and innovators who elevate the conversation and provide valuable insights. They help establish your community as the go-to space in your niche. These are the people who get a lot of "likes" for their contributions and are

sought after for their input. They may become the rock stars of your community.

CREATING THE FUTURE VISION

Now, with your ideal members firmly in mind, paint a vibrant, compelling picture of the transformation your community can facilitate. Use real stories, compelling examples, and authentic testimonials to make the journey feel tangible, desirable, and within reach.

When crafting your vision, consider the:

1. *Starting point:* What challenges or limitations are members facing right now? Acknowledge their current realities so they feel seen and understood. This builds empathy and supports trust.

2. *Destination:* What does success look like for your members? Use sensory-rich language to describe the outcomes they can expect, emotionally and practically. Let them visualize their future selves and let their fully imagined success drive their actions.

3. *Path:* How will your community guide members from where they are to where they want to be? Lay out the key steps, milestones, and support systems you'll provide. This can lower participants' anxiety, make them feel the journey is achievable, and add to their trusting the process and you.

CRAFTING YOUR COMMUNITY'S BIGGER PURPOSE

Armed with a clear understanding of your ideal members and the transformation you offer, it's time to distill your community's purpose into a memorable, actionable statement. Great, magnetic purpose statements include four key elements:

1. *Clarity:* It's easy to understand and share. Focus on simplicity and impact.

2. *Inspiration:* It sparks excitement, motivation, and a sense of possibility.

3. *Alignment:* It resonates with your ideal members' deepest desires and values.

4. *Invitation:* It welcomes people and invite them to play an active role. Use "we" language to create a sense of belonging.

Examples of powerful purpose statements:

• "We are a community of passionate innovators using cutting-edge AI tools to solve global challenges. Together, we are building a better future."

• "Our community exists to empower and connect heart-centered entrepreneurs. We believe in doing business with soul and substance."

• "Welcome to the movement of educators committed to infusing creativity into every classroom. Here, we reimagine what's possible in learning."

LIVING YOUR PURPOSE DAILY

A purpose is only powerful if it's woven into the fabric of your community. Here are some ways to **make your purpose tangible**:

• Reflect it in your content themes, challenges, and events. Every touchpoint should reinforce the journey.

• Highlight member stories that embody the transformation. Celebrate the small wins along the way.

- Bake it into your onboarding process. Welcome new members with a powerful reminder of the why.

- Encourage leaders and active members to become "purpose ambassadors." Equip them to inspire others.

PRACTICAL ACTIVITIES AND IMPLEMENTATION

Exercise:

1. Fill in the blanks. "Our community exists to [transformation you offer] for [ideal member] so they can [desired outcome]." Play with different wordings until you arrive at a purpose statement that feels electric.

2. Brainstorm three to five content themes, challenges, or events that align with and express your community's purpose. How could you make the purpose tangible and actionable?

3. Sketch out a "member journey map" showing the path from where your ideal members are currently to where your community will help them go. Consider the key milestones, emotional shifts, and aha moments along the way.

MEASURING SUCCESS, A.K.A. ALIGNMENT WITH PURPOSE

You need to decide early on how you will be measuring success. Metrics are essential for tracking your community's health and growth. Don't focus only on vanity numbers like post counts or log-in frequency. Measure the things that reflect progress toward reaching your purpose, such as:

- Member success stories and testimonials

- Engagement in purpose-driven activities or challenges

- Organic member referrals or social shares

- Positive sentiment in comments and conversations

- Growth in desired actions or outcomes, such as launches, collaborations, and more

GUIDING QUESTIONS

1. How does your community's purpose tap into something bigger than yourself? What broader vision or movement are you contributing to?

2. Imagine your community three years from now. What impact has it had on your members' lives? Write a vivid description of this future reality.

3. How will you ensure your purpose stays front and center as your community grows and evolves? What habits or rituals could you put in place to keep it alive?

4. What obstacles could I encounter when trying to define my community's purpose, and how can I overcome them?

5. What does my community's North Star look like? How would I describe it in detail when telling another person about my community?

PODCAST AND YOUTUBE RECOMMENDATIONS

NOTE: These podcasts and videos were accessible at the time of writing in March 2025. Not finding these exact episodes? Try finding similar content on YouTube.

- Simon Sinek's TED Talk, "How Great Leaders Inspire Action." This iconic talk introduces the concept of "Start with why" and the Golden Circle framework. Sinek explains how great leaders and organizations communicate from the inside out, starting with their purpose (why), proceeding to how they fulfill that purpose, and finally saying what they do. It's a perfect model for community builders seeking to articulate their core purpose.

- Brené Brown's The Call to Courage, a Netflix special. While technically a Netflix documentary, this powerful presentation explores how courage and vulnerability are essential to finding and living your purpose. Brown discusses how clarifying your values helps you make difficult decisions and stand firm in your convictions, critical skills for community leaders trying to maintain their North Star.

- The Community Strategy Podcast. Hosted by Deb Schell, this podcast features interviews with over 100 community leaders, business owners, and facilitators who share their community-building strategies. Deb is a community and marketing strategist who helps business owners develop and implement launch plans for online communities. You can find it on Apple podcasts and similar podcast platforms and at https://find-calmhere.com/podcast/

FAQS

1. How do I know if my community's purpose is strong enough?

A strong community purpose should resonate deeply with both you and your ideal members. It should be clear, concise, and inspire action. Ask yourself: Does it evoke a sense of passion and excitement? Does it address a genuine need or desire within your participants? Can it be easily understood? If your purpose feels vague, generic, or just uninspiring, it may need further refinement. Seek feedback from potential members and iterate until you have a purpose that ignites a shared vision.

2. **What if my ideal member profile is too broad?**

While it is tempting to try and appeal to everyone, a broad ideal member profile can lead to a diluted community experience. If your profile feels too broad, try to identify the core values, needs, and aspirations that unite your ideal members. Narrow your focus by considering demographics, psychographics, and specific interests. The more specific you are, the better you can tailor your content, activities, and overall community experience to meet their unique needs. Remember, it's better to have a smaller, highly engaged community than a large, disengaged one.

3. **How often should I revisit and refine our purpose?**

Your community's purpose should be a living document that evolves alongside your community. While the core values may remain consistent, the goals and objectives may need to be adjusted as your community grows and changes. It's a good practice to revisit and refine your purpose at least annually, or whenever you notice a shift in your community's dynamics or a change in your target audience's needs. Regularly seeking feedback from your members and staying attuned to their evolving needs will help you ensure that your community's purpose remains relevant and impactful

CHAPTER SUMMARY

In Chapter 2, we explored the critical role of purpose in building a thriving online community. We learned that a clear, compelling purpose acts as a North Star, guiding both the community's direction and its members' engagement. We also delved into the importance of understanding your ideal member's needs and aspirations, and how to craft a future vision that resonates deeply. By defining your ideal member and crafting a vision, you can start today building your kickass community

CHAPTER 2 WORKSHEET

Clarity of Purpose: Your Community's North Star

This worksheet is designed to help you clarify your community's purpose and create a strong foundation for your success. Complete the following sections to define your community's North Star.

SECTION A: DEFINING YOUR COMMUNITY'S PURPOSE

Identify the core elements.

Problem you're solving: *(What need does your community address?)*

_____

_____

People you're serving: *(Who is your ideal community member?)*

_____

_____

Transformation you're offering: *(What change will your community facilitate?)*

_____

_____

Unique approach: *(What makes your community different?)*

_____

_____

Craft your purpose statement. Combine the elements above into a clear, concise statement around the phrase, "our community."

Example: "Our community empowers aspiring writers to develop their craft, build confidence, and find publishing success through supportive workshops and peer group feedback."

_____

_____

_____

_____

SECTION B: ENVISIONING THE FUTURE TRANSFORMATION

Map the member's transformation journey:

Current state (challenges, struggles)	Bridge (how your community helps)	Future state (desired outcome)	What success looks like

Define indicators of success:
List specific, observable ways you'll know members are transforming.

SECTION C: CONNECTING WITH YOUR IDEAL MEMBER
Ideal member profile. Describe your ideal community member in detail.

Demographics (age, location, etc.):

Psychographics (values, interests, etc.):

Needs and aspirations:

Challenges:

SECTION D: COMMUNICATING YOUR PURPOSE

Reinforcement strategies.
How will you consistently communicate your community's purpose? Check all that apply:

☐   Welcome message

☐   Community guidelines

☐ Themed discussions and activities

☐ Member success stories

☐ Visual reminders (e.g., logo, slogan)

☐ Other: _____

Integration timeline.

Establish a timeline for integrating your purpose into your community's daily and weekly interactions.

Daily touchpoints: _____

Weekly rituals: _____

Monthly themes: _____

SECTION E: TESTING YOUR PURPOSE

Feedback and validation.

How will you gather feedback from potential and current members to ensure your purpose resonates?

_____

_____

_____

SECTION F: PURPOSE COMMUNICATION PLAN.

Ways to reinforce purpose (check ways you'll implement) the following:

☐ Welcome message

☐ Community guidelines

☐ Regular themed discussions

☐ Member success stories

☐ Visual reminders

☐ Other: _____

☐ Timeline for integration of purpose into:

Daily touchpoints _____

Weekly rituals _____

Monthly themes _____

SECTION G: LIVING YOUR PURPOSE

Decision-making filter
When faced with decisions, ask:

Does this align with our purpose?	☐ Yes	☐ No
Will this help members transform?	☐ Yes	☐ No
Does this strengthen our community?	☐ Yes	☐ No

Purpose review schedule
Set dates for:

Monthly review: _____

Quarterly assessment: _____

Annual purpose refresh: _____

LOOKING AHEAD

Now that you have your North Star shining bright, it's time to gather your community members around the campfire and create some magic. In Chapter 3, we'll explore how to spark engagement and build a vibrant community culture that brings your purpose to life through daily interactions, rituals, and shared experiences. Get ready to bring the heat!

BUILDING YOUR COMMUNITY CULTURE: THE CAMPFIRE OF CONNECTION

mission   vision   values

"We are all connected; To each other, biologically. To the earth, chemically. To the rest of the universe, atomically."

—Neil deGrasse Tyson, astrophysicist and science communicator

---

J ust as a campfire draws people in and creates a sense of warmth and connection, your community's culture has the power to turn a group of individuals into a tight-knit tribe. In the words of community pioneer Charles Vogl, "A community's culture is its life force. It's the invisible thread that weaves through every interaction, every decision, every moment of belonging."

The online community lives a similar life. Rosemary O'Neill, cofounder of Social Strata, makers of the Crowdstack community platform, explains: "Online community is not about building a website.

It's about building a home where your people want to stay." Building a kickass community culture requires intention, consistency, and a whole lot of heart. Let's dive into what it takes to create an environment where your members can thrive.

THE FOUNDATION: COMMUNITY CONNECTION

At the core of every strong community culture is a deep understanding of who belongs. Recall the member archetypes we explored in Chapter 2:

1. *Transformation seekers:* They're ready for change and growth. Your culture should provide the support and accountability they crave.

2. *Kindred spirits:* They share your passions and values. Your culture should give them a sense of home and connection.

3. *Action takers:* They're eager to contribute and make an impact. Your culture should provide opportunities for leadership and cocreation.

4. *Thought leaders:* They bring wisdom and expertise. Your culture should amplify their voices and ideas.

When you create a culture that speaks directly to the needs and desires of your ideal members, they can't help but feel a magnetic pull to belong. As Richard Millington, founder of FeverBee, eloquently puts it, "A community isn't a place or platform, it's a feeling. It's the feeling of belonging to a group of people who understand you."

CRAFTING YOUR COMMUNITY'S CULTURAL VISION

Like your community's purpose, your cultural vision should be clear, compelling, and memorable. It's the North Star that guides how your members show up and interact. Some key elements to consider:

1. *Shared values:* What principles and beliefs unite your members? These could be things like generosity, curiosity, inclusivity, or authenticity.

2. *Communication norms:* How do you want members to interact with each other? What tone and language reflect your community's personality?

3. *Rituals and traditions:* What regular practices or events will create a sense of shared experience and belonging? Think weekly check-ins, monthly challenges, or annual celebrations.

4. *Success stories:* What does transformation look like in your community? Highlight examples of members who embody the culture you're building.

When crafting your cultural vision, aim for something that's both aspirational and attainable. It should challenge your members to be their best selves while also feeling within reach. Venessa Paech, one of Australia's leading experts in online communities, reminds us that "great communities aren't built on rules and structure alone. They're built on stories, rituals, and shared experiences that create meaning."

MAKING YOUR CULTURE TANGIBLE

A cultural vision is powerful when it's woven into the daily life of your community. Here are some ways to make your culture real and relevant:

1. ***Onboarding and orientation:*** Welcome new members with a clear explanation of your community's values, norms, and rituals. Make them feel like insiders from day one. As Louise, an active member of Seth Godin's Purple Space community, advises, "Set community guidelines at the start." These guidelines need to be restated and reminders shared to keep behavior consistent. This need to remind members about guidelines came up frequently during my conversations with online community leaders.

2. ***Content and conversations:*** Infuse your cultural vision into the topics you discuss, the questions you ask, and the stories you share. Every touchpoint is an opportunity to reinforce what matters. Gina Bianchini, founder of Mighty Networks, captures this beautifully: "The best communities aren't built on content. They're built on connection. Content brings people in, but connection makes them stay."

3. ***Member spotlights and celebrations:*** Regularly highlight members who embody your community's culture. Celebrate their successes, their contributions, and their growth. As Louise and many others suggest, "Celebrate!"

4. ***Leadership and moderation:*** Ensure your team and key volunteers are culture champions. Equip them to model the norms and values you want to see in every interaction. In the wise words of Sam M., another Purple Space member, "When things go wrong, lean in and seek to understand." Leveraging the "calling in" culture highlighted by Loretta Ross's work, is immensely powerful and valuable. The idea is to call people in, instead of calling them out. Remain curious about who they are and what they are trying to share. Find ways to include your fellow members. Feelings of exclusion, or being called out, can hurt your community. This may be more of an art than an exact science, but it is a skill worth developing. Learning the art of calling in is essential to the success of healthy community building.

THE ART OF BELONGING

At the heart of every thriving community culture is a deep sense of belonging. It's the feeling that members matter, that they're seen and valued for who they are. Some ways to cultivate belonging include:

1. *Personalized interactions:* Use members' names, remember their stories, and tailor your responses to their unique needs and interests.

2. *Inclusive language:* Be mindful of the words you use. Avoid jargon, acronyms, or inside jokes that could make new members feel left out.

3. *Create a safe space:* Establish clear guidelines around respectful communication and confidentiality. Ensure that members feel psychologically safe to share vulnerably. Build trust with your members when they know you can be relied on for a response and will take steps needed to keep them all safe. Behaviors have consequences, and it is up to you to keep the community's healthy boundaries well maintained.

4. *Vulnerability and authenticity:* Lead by example. Share your own stories, challenges, and learning. Invite members to do the same. As Eva, a Purple Space participant, remarks, "Fostering a sense of belonging without sacrificing authenticity is the hard part. It starts with finding the right people to start with and creating guardrails against selfish behavior. Over time, the culture compounds."

GROWING WITH INTENTION

As your community grows and evolves, so, too, does its culture. The key is to stay intentional and proactive. Some tips:

1. ***Regular reflection:*** Set aside time to assess how well your community is living up to its cultural vision. Identify areas for improvement and celebration.

2. ***Member feedback:*** Regularly seek input from your members. What's working well? What could be better? What do they want more of?

3. ***Iteration and adaptation:*** Be willing to tweak and evolve your cultural practices over time. What worked for a hundred members may need to change for a thousand. As Louise wisely advises, "Add value, then add more."

4. ***Consistency and persistence:*** Building a strong culture takes time and repetition. Stay the course, even when it feels challenging. Don't give up. Your community is forgiving, and you can adjust course as needed. The payoff is worth it.

THE CULTURAL RHYTHM: CONSISTENCY THROUGH DESIGN

Monthly themes create a natural rhythm for your community. In January, you might focus on fresh starts and foundations. February could dive deep into building connections. This gives members a sense of progression and purpose.

An example might be weekly touchpoints like the following to keep the energy flowing:

- **Monday, member spotlights:** Kick off the week with inspiration.

- **Wednesday, wisdom:** Invite members to share insights and learnings

- **Friday, celebrations:** End the week on a high note with wins and gratitude

The key is consistency, members should know what to expect while still being delighted by the content itself.

Here's the real secret sauce: Celebration rituals. Remember Louise's wisdom: "When things go wrong, lean in and seek to understand." This approach, meeting challenges with curiosity instead of judgment, becomes part of your community's cultural DNA.

MEASURING CULTURAL HEALTH

How do you know if your culture is thriving? **Look for these signs:**

- Members reach out to help each other without prompting.

- Inside jokes and shared language emerge naturally and are explained to newbies.

- New members are welcomed warmly by existing members, not just moderators.

- Difficult conversations happen respectfully. Members are assuming the best of each other.

- Members bring their whole selves, not just their professional facades. They are asking vulnerable questions and providing brave and generous answers.

When you see these behaviors happening organically, you'll know your culture is alive and kicking. Some key metrics to track:

- Member retention and longevity
- Frequency and depth of member interactions

- Engagement in cultural rituals and traditions

- Sentiment analysis of member feedback

- Referral and advocacy rates (members inviting others to join)

THE ROAD AHEAD

Remember, building a strong culture is a **marathon, not a sprint**. It takes thirty to ninety days to lay the foundation. But the real magic unfolds over six to twelve months of consistent reinforcement. As Purple Space participant Eva Forde says, you'll need to repeat your values often. In her words: "People forget, and new people come in all the time."

Culture is your community's superpower. When done right, it creates a space within your community where people don't just show up. They show up excited, engaged, and ready to contribute. That's when you know you've built something truly kickass.

Practical application: Cultural development framework

1. Define core values.

    - What really matters to you?

    - What is important in the give and take of your community?

2. Create clear guidelines.

    - Communicate clearly, often, and repetitively what is expected of each community participant.

    - Specify consequences for not following guidelines.

    - Model appropriate behavior and use Loretta Ross's "calling in" techniques rather than shaming.

3. Establish key rituals.

   - Ensure that people are heard and take the time to listen and respond to others.

   - Encourage generous behavior.

   - Establish frameworks for requested feedback.

   - Honor when feedback is not requested.

4. Build recognition systems.

   - Consider gamification elements (emojis, icons, leaderboards).

   - Establish member recognition programs (member of the month, generosity awards).

   - Create opportunities to celebrate member achievements.

5. Measure cultural health.

   - Poll your community regularly.

   - Create a dashboard to track sentiment.

   - Use data to identify areas for adjustment or amplification

GUIDING QUESTIONS

1. Think of a community or group where you experienced a strong sense of belonging. What specific elements of the culture made you feel at home?

2. Imagine your community three to five years from now. What words would you want members to use when describing its culture to others?

3. How will you balance the need for consistency with the need for adaptability as your community grows and changes?

4. What specific transformation stories do you want your community to be known for?

5. How will your community's culture feel different from other spaces your members might join?

6. If someone were to visit your community for a day, what three feelings would you want them to walk away with? What specific cultural elements could you put in place to create those feelings?

PODCAST AND YOUTUBE RECOMMENDATIONS

> **NOTE:** These podcasts and videos were accessible at the time of writing in March 2025. Not finding these exact podcasts? Search for similar content on YouTube.

• For a deep dive into the art and science of belonging, check out the Community Signal podcast, with Patrick O'Keefe. The episode "Belonging: The Secret to Successful Communities," with Radha Agrawal is a must-listen.

• A must-read is Loretta Ross's excellent book, Calling In: How to Start Making Change With Those You'd Rather Cancel. It can be extraordinarily relevant to building your community. I refer to her framework and her perspective multiple times in this book.

• "The Culture Code" by Daniel Coyle on The Knowledge Project podcast is well worth a listen. In this episode, host Shane Parrish interviews Coyle about the key elements that create strong group identification. Coyle breaks down practical signals and behaviors that foster psychological safety, vulnerability, and purpose: all essential for intentionally cultivating community culture.

• Priya Parker's Ted Talk, "How to Create Meaningful Connections in a Remote World" is a must-see. The author of

The Art of Gathering, Parker shares insights about creating connection-rich environments, especially in virtual spaces. Parker discusses how thoughtful structure and intentional moments create cultural touchpoints that bring people together authentically.

FAQS

1. **How strict should community guidelines be?**

   Guidelines should be clear but not restrictive. Focus on what to do rather than what not to do. As award-winning Word Glue author Louise Karch advises, "Set community guidelines at the start," but ensure they enable rather than inhibit authentic connection.

2. **How do you handle members who don't align with the culture?**

   Start with a private conversation to understand their perspective. Use "calling in" as a methodology. If misalignment continues, it's okay to part ways respectfully. Remember that members have agreed to guidelines, and you need to follow through on consequences to maintain trust and safety.

3. **How long does it take to establish a strong culture?**

   While basic culture forms in the first thirty to ninety days, strong culture develops over six to twelve months of consistent reinforcement. Remember Eva's wisdom about repeating values "over and over because people forget, and new people come in all the time."

4. How do you maintain culture as you scale?

    Scale through small groups, maintain consistent rituals, and empower culture champions within the community. Document your culture code, and revisit it regularly with new members.

5. I'm worried about being too controlling with culture. How do I strike the right balance?

    Think of yourself as a gardener, not a drill sergeant. Create the right conditions for authentic connections to flourish, then let your members add their own flavor. Set clear boundaries around what's not acceptable, then leave plenty of room for organic growth.

CHAPTER SUMMARY

Culture requires intentional design and consistent nurturing. Be aware that your community's unique personality emerges through deliberate traditions, celebrations, and how you handle challenges. Strong culture takes six to twelve months to truly develop, but the foundation can be laid in thirty to ninety days. Keep in mind that regular reinforcement of values and expectations keeps your culture vibrant as your community grows. Success shows up in organic member interactions, natural peer support, and shared language.

In a world of anonymous online spaces, a strong culture isn't just nice to have, it's your secret power for creating a community that matters. The community's culture can be a source of pride to the members and what they talk about when they talk about their community. Let's give them something to talk about!

CHAPTER 3 WORKSHEET

Building Your Community Culture:
The Campfire of Connection

SECTION A: CULTURAL FOUNDATION

Core Values Compass

Define your top five community values and how they'll come to life.

Value	What It Means	How It Looks in Action
Example: Generosity	*Freely sharing knowledge without expectation*	*Daily help threads, resource libraries, celebrating others' wins*
1.		
2.		
3.		
4.		
5.		

Cultural Vision Statement

Complete this sentence: "In our community, members feel..."

_____

_____

_____

_____

SECTION B: MAKING CULTURE TANGIBLE

Community rituals
Design meaningful experiences that reinforce your values and create belonging.

Daily Touchpoints

Morning connection: _____

Support opportunities: _____

Celebration moments: _____

Weekly Rhythm

Monday: _____

Wednesday: _____

Friday: _____

Monthly Experiences

Theme focus: _____

Member spotlights: _____

Community celebrations: _____

SECTION C: THE ART OF BELONGING

Onboarding journey
Design their path from stranger to community insider.

First Twenty-four Hours

Personal welcome approach:

_____

Introduction invitation:

_____

First meaningful interaction:

_____

First Week

Values introduction method:

_____

Low-barrier participation opportunity:

_____

Connection points:

_____

First Month

Deeper engagement opportunity:

_____

Feedback checkpoint:

Recognition milestone:

Communication Toolkit
Craft key messages that bring your culture to life.

Welcome message template:

Community guidelines summary:

"How we roll" overview:

SECTION D: GROWING WITH INTENTION

Quarterly Theme Plan
Map your first season of community experiences.

Quarter one focus.

Month one theme:

Month two theme:

Month three theme:

Success indicators.

Member engagement metric:

_____

Cultural adoption sign:

_____

Growth benchmark:

_____

Community Health Dashboard

Track the following indicators to ensure your culture is thriving.

Cultural health indicator	Current base-line	Ninety-day goal
Active participation rate		
Members helping members (weekly instances)		
New member retention (thirty days)		
Response time to questions		
Member-initiated conversations		
Member satisfaction score		

SECTION E: PROTECTING YOUR CULTURE

Community Guidelines
List your friendly-but-firm nonnegotiables.

1. _____

2. _____

3. _____

4. _____

5. _____

"Calling In"
Document your approach for addressing challenging behavior with compassion.

Private conversation triggers:

_____

Helpful language template:

_____

Follow-up process:

_____

Consequences framework:

_____

SECTION F: SCALING WITH SOUL

Culture Champions Program

Selection criteria:

Training elements:

Responsibilities:

Recognition approach:

Small-Group Strategy

As you grow, how will you maintain intimacy?

Ideal group sizes:

Connection mechanisms:

Cross-group opportunities:

SECTION G: IMPLEMENTATION PLAN

Next Steps:

1. _____

2. _____

3. _____

Thirty-day culture launch

Week one priority:

_____

Week two priority:

_____

Week three priority:

_____

Week four priority:

_____

Quarterly Culture Check-in
Schedule your first culture review.

Date: _____

REMINDER: Culture isn't something you create once and check off your list. It is something you nurture every day through consistent actions, thoughtful leadership, and intentional design. Yes, it does take effort, and yes, the payoff will be significant if you do this correctly. Your community culture is your greatest competitive advantage and the heart of what makes your space special. Make it kickass!

LOOKING AHEAD

Now that you've laid the foundation for a vibrant community culture, it's time to explore who will tend that cultural flame. A thriving culture requires intentional leadership, the kind that both embodies your community's values and empowers others to do the same.

Think of your community culture as a garden you've carefully designed. The seeds are planted, the vision is clear, and for it to flourish, you need skilled gardeners who understand both the science and art of growth. These are your community leaders.

In Chapter 4, we'll explore how to identify, develop, and support the leaders who will bring your cultural vision to life. You'll learn how to:

- Identify and nurture leadership potential within your existing community.

- Create leadership structures that scale as your community grows.

- Empower leaders with the right balance of autonomy and guidance.

- Foster a leadership approach that reinforces your cultural values at every level.

As community strategist David Spinks notes, "The most successful communities are those where leadership is distributed, not centralized." The culture you've designed provides the blueprint. Now it's time to assemble the team that will build something extraordinary. Let's continue to discover how purpose-driven leadership transforms a good community into an exceptional one.

Ready to dive deeper? Find me on LinkedIn and let's make your community culture legendary.

LEADING WITH PURPOSE AND IMPACT: THE ART OF EMPOWERING OTHERS

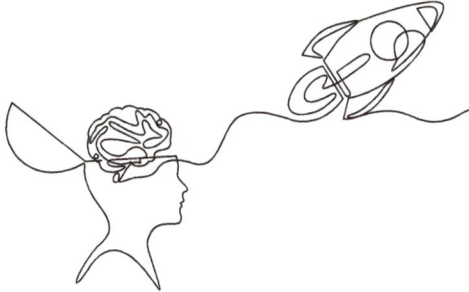

"A community isn't a place or platform; it's a feeling. It's the feeling of belonging to a group of people who understand you."

—Gina Bianchini, founder of Mighty Networks

I n the digital landscape we navigate today, effective community leadership has undergone a profound transformation. The old command-and-control approach has given way to something far more powerful: leadership that empowers, elevates, and enables others to shine. As Keith, an active member

Gina Bianchini

of Seth Godin's Purple Space community, eloquently puts it: "It's a balanced community. When I show up, 'I'm not thinking I'm getting something in return, and Purple Space isn't trying to extract value out of me. It's all generative.'"

This is the secret sauce of kickass community leadership: Creating community spaces where value explodes like fireworks, authentic, electric, and difficult to fake. You're not just leading; you're igniting a chain reaction of awesomeness! Think of yourself as the conductor of the world's most badass orchestra, unleashing each player's unique superpowers so they can riff, jam, and create mind-blowing symphonies together. When you nail this, your community doesn't just hum, it roars.

THE FOUR PILLARS OF COMMUNITY LEADERSHIP

Effective community leadership rests on four essential pillars working together to create thriving, vibrant spaces:

1. Visionary direction

Great community leaders don't just manage the present; they illuminate the path forward. This isn't about crafting a fancy mission statement that collects dust. It's about painting such a vivid picture of where you're headed that your members can see and taste it.

When you talk about transformation, make it tangible. Don't just say, "We help entrepreneurs succeed." Spell out exactly what that success looks like, feels like, and sounds like. Share stories of what's possible. Create content that showcases the journey and the destination. Bring the passion!

As Jono Bacon, a seasoned community strategist, notes: "The most successful communities don't just share information, they share a journey. They're working together toward something meaningful."

2. Generous facilitation

Real leadership happens in the posts and comments and shares, in the day-to-day interactions that build trust and connection. It's about:

- Asking thoughtful questions instead of rushing to provide answers.

- Creating spaces where members can showcase their expertise.

- Connecting people who could benefit from knowing each other.

- Highlighting insights and contributions from across the community.

Well-known community consultant, Carrie Melissa Jones, tells us: "The magic happens when you stop trying to be the star of the show and start being the host of the party. Great community leaders create space for others to shine."

This shift from holding the spotlight to shining the spotlight on others, transforms the entire dynamic of your community. When members see that their contributions matter, they invest more deeply, engage more authentically, and commit more fully to the community's success.

3. Consistent nurturing

Think of your community like a living organism. It has some basic requirements such as a heartbeat, a rhythm that members can feel and anticipate. This rhythm comes from intentional nurturing. I mentioned this in the previous chapter as an important component of your community's culture. Here, it is a component of your impactful leadership. This is about leading intentional activities and weaving your vision into these recurring engagements.

We mentioned **monthly themes**, **weekly touchpoints**, and **daily habits**. Be sure to find ways for them to elevate your vision and leverage them as a leadership approach for how you want to see event-building in your community.

For example: **Weekly touchpoints** can also be used to both maintain momentum and build your engagement vision.

- **Monday:** Motivation kicks things off with inspiration, giving a boost of energy to your team, and letting them feel your presence.

- **Wednesday:** Wins celebrate progress and milestones, and guide people over the hump, letting them know more events might be happening later in the week.

- **Friday:** Reflections capture learning and growth. What did you ship this week? Who are you grateful for this week? In Purple Space, we have a weekly prompt on these two generous topics: one about getting work done and acknowledged, and another based on generously expressing gratitude to specific members.

- **Weekend challenges:** These can be used to push members just beyond their comfort zones. Did anyone join? Make sure you follow up and see what evolved.

Daily habits are where the magic happens, potentially including morning check-ins, support threads, moments of recognition. These small, consistent actions weave the fabric of your community.

David Spinks, cofounder of the community business CMX, reminds us: "Community building is not about gathering people for the sake of gathering them. It's about creating spaces where people can achieve things together that they couldn't achieve alone."

4. Distributed empowerment

The final pillar, and perhaps the most transformative, is the ability to identify, nurture, and empower other leaders within your community. This isn't just about preventing your own burnout—though that's a significant benefit. It's about creating a resilient community that can thrive beyond any single person's involvement.

Look for members who naturally:

- Welcome newcomers without being asked.

- Answer questions helpfully and promptly.

- Consistently show up with positive energy.

- Embody the values and culture you've established.

Start small. Maybe potential leaders host a weekly thread or moderate a specific discussion. As they grow, so can their responsibilities. Before you know it, you've got a leadership team that makes your community even stronger than you could have made it alone.

FROM SOLO LEADER TO LEADERSHIP ECOSYSTEM

Let me tell you about Sara (not her real name). She joined an online community as a quiet member, occasionally commenting on posts. The community leaders noticed how thoughtfully she responded to others, how she remembered details about people's journeys. They invited her to host a weekly coffee chat. Those chats became member favorites. Today, Sara runs multiple community initiatives, and her leadership style has inspired a whole new wave of emerging leaders.

The key? The community leaders didn't wait for Sara to raise her hand. They saw her potential and created space for it to grow.

This evolution from solo leadership to a leadership ecosystem follows a natural progression.

Phase one. Foundational leadership

You're doing most of the heavy lifting, posting content, answering questions, welcoming new members. This is necessary at the start, and probably not sustainable over the long term.

Phase two. Participatory leadership

You begin to invite active members into specific roles, perhaps moderating certain discussions or helping with onboarding. You're still the primary leader, but you're no longer the only leader.

Phase three. Distributed leadership

Various aspects of the community are now led by different members. You provide guidance and support, but the community has developed its own momentum and leadership capacity.

Phase four. Ecosystem leadership

The community now functions as a vibrant ecosystem with multiple leaders at various levels. New leaders emerge naturally, and leadership development happens organically within the community itself.

Howard Rheingold, a pioneer in virtual communities, expresses the journey like this: "The technology of online communities is interesting, but the human potential is revolutionary."

THE MONEY TALK (WE NEED TO HAVE IT)

Let's talk about the value exchange of monetization. The reality is that financial investment creates meaningful commitment, people engage more deeply with what they've paid to access. However, not all monetization approaches serve your community equally well. There's a delicate balance between creating sustainable revenue and preserving the authentic connection that makes your community thrive in the first place. Plus, there are differing perspectives on this hot topic. Some say build value first. Prove your worth. Then create pricing tiers that feel like a no-brainer because the transformation is so clear:

- **Core membership:** Daily support and access to the community

- **Premium experiences:** Deeper learning opportunities or specialized programs

- **High-touch options:** More personalized guidance or mentorship

Others recommend pricing appropriately up front because people pay attention to and value what they pay for, although this isn't consistently true if we look at gym membership. Think about what makes the most sense for you and your community, what is most appropriate for your values. I have successfully started communities both ways.

Rosemary O'Neill of Social Strata aptly puts it this way: "Online community is not about building a website. It's about building a home where your people want to stay." Focus on creating a space that's so valuable, so transformative that members can't imagine not being a part of it.

The monetization conversation will continue in the next chapters. This conversation and the understanding of monetization usually evolves over time.

LEADING THROUGH CHALLENGES

Even the most thriving communities face challenges. How you navigate these moments defines your leadership more than how you handle success:

Challenge one: The crickets phase

Every community experiences periods when engagement drops. Great leaders don't panic, they innovate. Try these:

- Personally reaching out to previously active members.

- Introducing a fresh discussion format or challenge.

- Being transparent and asking for feedback about what would spark more engagement.

Challenge two: Difficult dynamics

When conflicts arise or someone consistently disrupts the community vibe, effective leaders:

- Address issues privately before they become public problems.

- Establish clear boundaries while maintaining respect.

- Model the communication style they want to see in the community.

Challenge three: Scaling growing pains

As your community grows, maintaining intimacy becomes challenging. Navigate this by:

- Creating subgroups around specific interests or goals.

- Developing a clear onboarding process that conveys a culture.

- Empowering more leaders to maintain the personal touch.

FeverBee's Richard Millington observes that "the best communities don't scale by getting bigger; they scale by getting deeper."

Practical application: Leadership development framework

1. Define your leadership philosophy

    - What core values guide your leadership approach?
    - How do you balance structure with flexibility?
    - What does empowerment look like in practical terms?

2. Create your community rhythm

    - Establish consistent touchpoints (daily, weekly, monthly).
    - Design engagement rituals that reinforce community values.
    - Build recognition systems that celebrate member contributions.

3. Develop your leadership pipeline

- Identify potential leaders based on natural behaviors.
- Create progressive responsibility opportunities.
- Establish mentorship relationships between current and emerging leaders.

4. Implement feedback systems

- Regular community health assessments
- Anonymous feedback options
- Transparent sharing of what's working and what needs adjustment

5. Build resilience planning

- Emergency response procedures for community crises
- Leadership backup systems for continuity
- Self-care practices to prevent burnout

THE PATH OF PERSONAL LEADERSHIP GROWTH

Your community can only grow as much as you do. Commit to your own leadership development through:

- **Regular reflection** about what's working and what could be improved. Checking in with yourself is essential. It is where your personal growth happens. Find out what works best for your personal check-ins; a regular schedule, meditation, journaling are all legit options.

- **Seeking mentorship** from those who are further along in their leadership journey. This includes joining other generous communities and discussing issues with peers. Attending relevant conferences can also be beneficial.

- **Building a peer network** of other community leaders for support and sharing ideas.

- **Investing in learning** through books, courses, podcasts, YouTube videos, and topic-specific webinars and conferences.

Remember that leadership isn't a destination but a journey of continuous growth and adaptation. Each challenge you face is an opportunity to deepen your leadership capacity.

MEASURING LEADERSHIP IMPACT

Track these key metrics to gauge your leadership effectiveness:

- **Member engagement rates:** Are people actively participating?

- **Retention metrics:** Are members staying and deepening their commitment?

- **Leadership development:** How many active leaders are emerging within the community?

- **Sentiment analysis:** What's the emotional tone of member interactions and feedback?

- **Goal achievement:** Is the community making progress toward its stated purpose?

- **Autonomy indicators:** How many valuable discussions happen without your direct involvement?

GUIDING QUESTIONS

1. Think about a leader who has had a profound impact on your life. What specific qualities or actions made them so effective?

How can you embody those qualities in your own community leadership?

2. Imagine your community three years from now. What role do you want to be playing? What role do you want your members to be playing? What needs to happen between now and then to make that a reality?

3. What's one thing you're currently doing as a leader that you could delegate or automate? How would that free you up to focus on higher-impact activities?

4. What's one leadership responsibility you're currently holding onto that could be an opportunity for a member to grow.

5. Consider a recent challenge in your community. How did your leadership approach influence the outcome? What might you do differently next time?

PODCAST AND YOUTUBE RECOMMENDATIONS

> **NOTE:** These podcasts and videos were accessible at the time of writing in March 2025. Not finding these exact episodes? Search for similar content on YouTube.

- Tune into Conversations with Bacon for the episode on YouTube that's a masterclass in community engagement and to hear Jono Bacon provide an example about leadership. You'll find the episode at https://youtu.be/FT4IhKoAbIE?si=1-UhrfKOUqsFwCpL.

- Watch the YouTube video of "How to Lead: Turning Followers into Leaders," a TED Talk by David Marquet. This compelling talk from Marquet, a former submarine commander, explores his journey from giving orders to creating leaders at every level. His practical framework for intent-based leadership shows exactly how to empower community members to step up and lead from wherever they are. See it at: https://youtu.be/ivwKQqf4ixA?si=b14SiPYPxw0BvCqa

- Explore the Akimbo podcast by Seth Godin. Any podcast featuring Seth Godin is worth your time—his conversations with Gina Bianchini and Tim Ferriss are particularly insightful. But you'll discover that his own podcast, Akimbo, repeatedly explores leadership themes that resonate deeply with community builders. The episodes "Leadership Jazz" and "Organizing the Unorganized" are particularly relevant for those looking to lead with both purpose and impact.

FAQS

1. **How do I know if I'm being too hands-on or not hands-on enough?**

   Watch your community's independence level. If most discussions need your input to keep going, you might be too central. If people feel lost or unsupported, you might need to be more present. Aim for a state where your members initiate and sustain engagement while you provide direction and support.

2. **When should I start looking for additional leaders?**

   Day one. Keep a running list of members who show leadership potential through their natural behaviors and contributions. Leadership development should be an ongoing process, not something you start when you're already feeling overwhelmed.

3. **How do I maintain quality as I delegate leadership?**

   Create clear guidelines, provide training, and keep communication channels open. Regular check-ins help maintain standards while empowering others to lead. Remember that different leaders will bring their own style and strengths. This diversity strengthens your community.

4. **How do I handle a situation where a community leader isn't working out?**

   Address it promptly but privately. Start with curious questions rather than accusations. Perhaps there's a mismatch between their strengths and their current role, or they need additional support. If necessary, create a graceful transition plan that maintains their dignity while protecting the community experience.

5. **How transparent should I be about business decisions affecting the community?**

   Err on the side of transparency. Members appreciate being treated as partners rather than consumers. When changes need to happen, explaining the why behind decisions builds trust and understanding, even when the changes might not be universally popular.

CHAPTER SUMMARY

Leading a kickass community isn't about being the star of the show, it's about creating environments where others can shine. Remember the four pillars of community leadership, visionary direction, generous facilitation, consistent nurturing, and distributed empowerment? By embracing them, you create the conditions for transformative growth.

Your most important role is to be the conductor. When you lead with purpose and heart, you create a space where everyone can thrive. Your leadership approach sets the tone for everything that happens in your community, so lead with intention, authenticity, and a genuine desire to see others succeed.

CHAPTER 4 WORKSHEET

Leading With Purpose and Impact

SECTION A: LEADERSHIP FOUNDATION

Your Leadership Profile

Rate yourself (1–5) in these areas.

_____ Visionary direction (*creating and communicating a compelling vision*)

_____ Generous facilitation (*helping others contribute their best*)

_____ Consistent cultivation (*maintaining community rhythm*)

_____ Distributed empowerment (*developing other leaders*)

_____ Adaptability (*responding effectively to challenges*)

_____ Authentic connection (*building genuine relationships*)

_____ Setting boundaries (*maintaining healthy community standards*)

Leadership Philosophy Statement

Complete the following prompts. As a community leader, I will...

Empower others by: _____

Create value through: _____

Build trust by: _____

Measure success via: _____

Navigate challenges through: _____

SECTION B: COMMUNITY RHYTHM DESIGN

Monthly Themes Planning
Map out your first three months.

Month one

Theme: _____

Key content pieces: _____

Community activities: _____

Growth objective: _____

Month two

Theme: _____

Key content pieces: _____

Community activities: _____

Growth objective: _____

Month three

Theme: _____

Key content pieces: _____

Community activities: _____

Growth objective: _____

Weekly Touchpoints Framework
Design your ideal week.

Monday

Morning ritual: _____

Main content or activity: _____

Engagement goal: _____

Wednesday

Morning ritual: _____

Main content or activity: _____

Engagement goal: _____

Friday

Morning ritual: _____

Main content or activity: _____

Engagement goal: _____

Daily Leadership Routines

Morning

Community check-in: _____

Priority review: _____

Member recognition: _____

Afternoon

Engagement check: _____

Support response: _____

Leadership tasks: _____

Evening

Day summary: _____

Tomorrow prep: _____

Celebration notes: _____

SECTION C: LEADERSHIP DEVELOPMENT PIPELINE

Identification of Potential Leaders
Identify members showing leadership qualities.

Name	
Strengths	
Potential	
Next Step	

Name	
Strengths	
Potential	
Next Step	

Name	
Strengths	
Potential	
Next Step	

Name	
Strengths	
Potential	
Next Step	

Leadership Roles Framework
Define progressive leadership opportunities.

Entry-level roles

1. _____

2. _____

3. _____

Intermediate roles

1. _____

2. _____

3. _____

Advanced roles

1. _____

2. _____

3. _____

Leadership Training Plan
How will you develop your leaders?

Onboarding Process

1. _____
2. _____
3. _____

Ongoing Development

1. _____
2. _____
3. _____

Recognition System

1. _____
2. _____
3. _____

SECTION D: COMMUNICATION STRATEGY

Key Message Templates
Create templates for common communications.

Community Update Templates

Hey [community name] members!

Here's what's happening this week: [key event or activity] [important announcement] [member spotlight]:

Congratulations to [name] for [achievement]. What we're focusing on: [weekly theme or topic].

Question of the week: [engaging question]. Looking forward to connecting with all of you!

[your name]

Member Recognition

A special shout-out to [member name]! [he/she/they] has/have been an incredible part of our community by [specific contribution or achievement]. This perfectly embodies our [relevant community value]. Please join me in celebrating [name]'s impact!

You can create your own templates for other areas such as Challenges and Guideline Reminders. Creating and leveraging systems will help streamline your community management processes.

Feedback Systems Design
How will you gather and implement feedback?

Regular Check-ins

Member surveys (frequency):

_____

One-on-one conversations (with whom and when):

_____

Group feedback sessions (format and frequency):

_____

Feedback Implementation Process.

Please describe what you believe is the best way.

_____

_____

_____

_____

_____

SECTION E: CRISIS MANAGEMENT PREPARATION

Common Challenges Response Plan

Challenge type	Prevention strategy	Response approach	Follow-up process
Low engagement			
Conflict between members			
Toxic behavior			
Platform issues			

Leadership Continuity Plan
Ensure community thrives, even when you're unavailable.

Critical Functions

Function	Primary person	Backup person	Documentation location

Emergency Communication Plan

1. _____

2. _____

3. _____

SECTION F: MONETIZATION STRATEGY (IF APPLICABLE)

Value Proposition Clarity
What specific transformation does your community offer?

For Free or Basic Members:

1. _____

2. _____

3. _____

For Premium Members:

1. _____

2. _____

3. _____

For High-Touch Offerings:

1. _____

2. _____

3. _____

Design of Pricing Structure

Base this on the value delivered, not just market rates.

	Name	Price	Includes
Tier 1			
Tier 2			
Tier 3			

SECTION G: PERSONAL LEADERSHIP DEVELOPMENT

Growth Areas

Identify your top three leadership development priorities.

1. _____

2. _____

3. _____

Learning Plan

Skill to develop	Resources needed	Timeline	Success Metric

Support System

Who will help you grow as a leader?

Mentor(s): _____

Peer community: _____

Coach or adviser: _____

Accountability partner: _____

SECTION H: IMPLEMENTATION TIMELINE

Thirty-day Leadership Focus

Week one: Set up systems

Monday: _____

Tuesday: _____

Wednesday: _____

Thursday: _____

Friday: _____

Week two: Team development

Key focus: _____

Primary tasks: _____

Success indicators: _____

Week three: Implementation of communication

Key focus: _____

Primary tasks: _____

Success indicators: _____

Week four: Review and adjust

Assessment approach: _____

Celebration plan: _____

Preparation for next month: _____

Leadership vision statement

In one paragraph, describe the leader you aspire to be and the impact you want to have on your community.

LOOKING AHEAD

Now that you've established a strong leadership foundation for your community, it's time to focus on turning vision into action: meaningful member engagement. Even the most inspired leadership means little without consistent, purposeful interaction among your members.

Think of your leadership as the scaffolding that supports your community's structure. With that framework firmly in place, it's time to turn our attention to the heartbeat of your community—the daily exchanges, conversations, and connections that transform a group of individuals into a vibrant collective.

In Chapter 5, we'll dive into proven strategies for sparking meaningful engagement. You'll discover how to:

• Design irresistible conversation starters that ignite genuine interaction.

• Create engagement rituals that members eagerly anticipate.

- Structure activities that deepen relationships between members.

- Balance content consumption with active participation.

- Overcome the dreaded crickets phase that every community faces.

As Richard Millington notes, "The most engaged [community members] aren't engaging with you; they're engaging with each other." You've built the foundation as a leader; now it's time to create the conditions for your members to build relationships with one another.

Go ahead and explore the art and science of community engagement, where your leadership and vision is transformed into a living, breathing community. Let's keep the energy high. Get ready to bring the heat!

Ready to dive deeper? Find me on LinkedIn, and let's make your community culture legendary.

ENGAGEMENT ARCHITECTURE: BUILDING PARTICIPATION THAT MATTERS

"The best communities aren't built on content; they're built on connection. Content brings people in, but connection makes them stay."

—Gina Bianchini, founder of Mighty Networks

When you walk into a room buzzing with electric energy, that's the power of engagement in action. That's the feeling we're aiming to create in your online community. Not just aimless chatter or superficial interactions, but real, substantial participation that has members thinking, "I can't imagine not being a part of this." We want to create engagements that matter to the participants.

Keith, an active member of Seth Godin's Purple Space community, perfectly captures this sentiment: "When you have a community like Purple, for me, it's more [about] actually communing and connecting. That's why I'm still there." Notice how he doesn't mention fancy features or flashy content. For Keith, it's all about the **depth of connection.**

In this chapter, we're diving deep into the architecture of engagement, the intentional design of experiences, interactions, and systems that transform passive observers into active, committed participants. This isn't about tricks or gimmicks; it's about creating an environment where meaningful participation feels natural, rewarding, and essential.

THE ENGAGEMENT PYRAMID: FROM LURKING TO LEADING

All community engagement exists on a spectrum. Understanding this hierarchy helps you design experiences that meet members where they are while gently encouraging them to climb higher:

Level 1: Consumption

Members read posts, watch videos, and absorb content without actively participating. This is where most members start.

Engagement goal: Make consumption valuable enough that they want to return, but incomplete enough that they feel drawn to participate.

Level 2: Reaction

Members take micro-actions, like liking posts, voting in polls, or using emojis to express themselves. These are low-risk ways to start participating.

Engagement goal: Acknowledge these small interactions to reinforce the behavior and invite deeper participation.

Level 3: Contribution

Members actively post comments, answer questions, and share ideas. This is where real dialogue begins.

Engagement goal: Create safe, structured opportunities for contribution with clear prompts and positive reinforcement.

Level 4: Collaboration

Members begin working together on projects, forming accountability partnerships, or participating in group challenges.

Engagement goal: Facilitate relationships between members and highlight successful collaborations.

Level 5: Creation

Members initiate discussions, create content, organize events, or lead initiatives within the community.

Engagement goal: Empower creative leadership with resources, recognition, and runway to experiment.

As Venessa Paech, a seasoned community professional, reminds us, "Great communities aren't built on rules and structure alone. They're built on stories, rituals, and shared experiences that create meaning."

THE SECRET SAUCE OF TRUE ENGAGEMENT

An unfortunate reality is that posting a dozen "engagement questions" daily isn't a recipe for meaningful interaction; it's a recipe for noise. True engagement happens when members feel so connected to the community's purpose and people that participating becomes as natural as breathing.

Think about building your community's engagement like hosting a dinner party that never ends. You wouldn't just toss random conversation starters at your guests every five minutes. Instead, you'd create an environment where conversations flow organically, where inside jokes develop, and where people feel comfortable enough to share both victories and vulnerabilities. It is okay to provide some relevant prompts, but, as Jono Bacon recommends, remember to do it intentionally and mindfully. Create a conversation that connects your community and isn't just static noise.

The secret sauce combines five essential ingredients.

1. Purpose-driven interaction

Every engagement opportunity should connect back to your community's core purpose. Whether it's a discussion prompt, an event, or a challenge, members should understand how participation moves them closer to the transformation they seek.

Implementation tactic: For each engagement activity you design, explicitly state how it connects to your community's purpose. For example: "This week's challenge is designed to help you overcome the perfectionism that's blocking your creative output."

2. Psychological safety

Members need to feel that their contributions will be respected, not ridiculed. This safety isn't about avoiding challenging conversations; it's about ensuring those conversations happen with respect and good faith.

Implementation tactic: Model vulnerability by sharing your own challenges and lessons learned. When members take risks by sharing, acknowledge their courage specifically: "Thank you for sharing that difficult experience, Sophie. That kind of honesty helps all of us grow."

3. Social proof

Members are naturally drawn to participate when they observe engagement from peers they admire or feel connected to, creating a powerful ripple effect throughout the community.

Implementation tactic: Strategically highlight diverse examples of participation. "Last week, we had amazing insights from newcomer James, longtime member Sarah, and quiet observer Alex, who spoke up for the first time!" Using their names, knowing they might get this name recognition, goes a long way.

4. Progressive challenge

Engagement should start simple and gradually increase in depth and vulnerability as trust builds.

Implementation tactic: Design engagement pathways that evolve over time. Week one might ask for simple introductions, while week six invites' members to share their biggest professional struggles.

5. Meaningful recognition

Acknowledgment of contribution fuels further engagement, especially when it highlights the specific impact of a member's participation.

Implementation tactic: Move beyond generic "thanks for sharing" to specific recognition, such as, "Your question about client boundaries sparked our most valuable discussion this month and helped at least five members rethink their policies."

As Richard Millington of FeverBee notes, "A community isn't a place or platform, it's a feeling. It's the feeling of belonging to a group of people who understand you."

BUILDING YOUR ENGAGEMENT ENGINE

Let's get practical about how to create this kind of engagement magic. Your community needs a rhythm, a heartbeat that members can feel and anticipate. Here's how you can organize it.

Daily Touchpoints

As previously mentioned, these small but consistent interactions keep your community feeling alive and active:

- **Morning rituals:** Start the day with a check-in question that takes less than 30 seconds to answer but creates a sense of presence. "What's your focus today?" or "Share your mood in three words." Or potentially share a prompt.

- **Celebration spots:** Designate places for quick wins and mini celebrations. "Hit a milestone? Drop it here!" These small victories create positive energy that fuels deeper engagement.

Emojis are acceptable as responsible and can enliven a flat environment.

- **Support threads:** Create dedicated spaces for asking questions where members know they'll get helpful, judgment-free responses. "Your safety place to ask for support 24/7."

> **PRO TIP:** Vary your posting times to accommodate different time zones and schedules. Platforms like Circle and Mighty Networks allow you to schedule posts in advance.

Weekly Rhythms

These become the anchors of your community calendar that members begin to anticipate and look forward to.

- **Monday member spotlights:** Kick-start the week by celebrating your community's rockstars. Don't just highlight their achievements; dig into their journey, challenges, and what they've learned along the way.

- **Wednesday wisdom:** Create a midweek knowledge-sharing ritual where members can share their expertise, resources, or lessons learned. This positions your community as a valuable learning resource.

- **Friday reflections:** Help everyone process the week's insights and aha moments. "What did you learn this week that surprised you?" or "What's one thing you'll do differently next week based on what you learned?" Or "Share your gratitude for a community member's contribution."

> **PRO TIP:** Don't just post these prompts and disappear. Engage with the responses. Ask follow-up questions. Connect members who might be able to help each other. Be the dinner party host who makes sure everyone's having a great time.

Monthly Themes

These give your community a sense of direction and progression that keeps members invested in the longer journey. Although mentioned before, I'm noting these repeat actions here as well. This is your engagement chapter, and these weekly processes can create your foundation for engagement. Also, repeating this might help this perspective stick!

- **Thematic focus:** Maybe January explores "clarity and vision," while February tackles "building systems that scale." These themes create a shared journey that keeps members invested.

- **Skill-building challenges:** Organize thirty-day challenges around your monthly theme. For February's systems theme, members might commit to documenting one business process each week.

- **Panels of experts:** Bring in guests who can speak to the monthly theme, offering fresh perspectives and specialized knowledge.

  PRO TIP: Announce the next month's theme a week in advance to build anticipation. Create a simple visual graphic for each theme that members can save or even use as their device wallpaper.

As David Spinks says, "Community is not about gathering people for the sake of gathering them. It's about creating spaces where people can achieve things together that they couldn't achieve alone."

SEVEN ENGAGEMENT FORMATS THAT WORK

Many communities fall into the trap of using the same engagement formats over and over until members tune out. Let's explore seven proven formats that you can mix and match to keep your community fresh and engaging:

1. The hot seat

One member presents a specific challenge or question, and the community focuses their collective wisdom on helping that person. This creates deep value for the featured member while showcasing the community's expertise.

> **EXAMPLE:** "This week's Hot Seat features Maria's content strategy dilemma. Drop your best advice, resources, or questions to help her reach her ideal audience!"

2. Peer challenges

Members commit to a specific action or habit for a set period, with regular check-ins to share progress and obstacles. The accountability and shared experience create strong bonds.

> **EXAMPLE:** "Join our 21-day pitch perfect challenge! Commit to sending one outreach email daily and report back on your results. Templates and support provided!"

3. Rapid-fire roundtables

Time-limited discussions on specific topics with clear participation guidelines. The constraint of time creates energy and focused contribution.

> **EXAMPLE:** "Today's thirty-minute roundtable: client onboarding hacks. Drop your best tip, tool, or template. We'll compile the top ideas into a resource guide!"

4. Experience sharing

Structured prompts that invite members to share personal experiences related to a specific topic. These create empathy and connection through storytelling.

> **EXAMPLE:** "Share your origin story. What unexpected twist or turn led you to your current work? What seemed like a setback that turned out to be a blessing?"

5. Resource exchanges

Dedicated threads where members can share and request specific tools, templates, or resources. These create immediate practical value while positioning members as helpful experts.

> **EXAMPLE:** "April resource exchange. What's one tool or template that's saved you hours of work? What are you looking for help with this month?"

6. Celebration rituals

Structured ways to acknowledge milestones, victories, and progress. These reinforce the community's supportive culture and highlight the tangible benefits of membership.

> **EXAMPLE:** Monthly victory vault. "Share one thing you accomplished this month that you're proud of. Bonus: Tell us how this community supported you along the way."

7. Expert AMAs (Ask-Me-Anythings)

Scheduled sessions where a member or guest expert answers community questions on their area of expertise. These create high-value content while showcasing the diverse knowledge within your community.

> **EXAMPLE:** "This Thursday at 1 p.m. ET: Email marketing AMA with our own Sophia Chen. Bring your burning questions about list-building, segmentation, or crafting subject lines that get clicks!"

The key to making these formats successful is thoughtful facilitation. Set clear expectations, model the type of participation you want to see, and actively guide the conversation to keep it valuable and on track.

CASE STUDY: THE THIRTY-DAY ENGAGEMENT CHALLENGE

Let me tell you about a community that took these principles and created dramatic results. Instead of just posting endless threads and hoping for engagement, they designed a structured, thirty-day challenge to transform lurkers into active contributors.

The setup:

- Clear expectations were set at the beginning. "Just 5 minutes a day for thirty days to transform your experience in this community."

- A simple tracking system where members could see their progress and get recognition for consistency.

- Graduated challenges that started with low-risk participation and gradually increased in depth.

The schedule:

- **Days 1–7: Foundation.** Simple personal sharing to establish presence (introduce yourself, share your workspace, describe your ideal day)

- **Days 8–14: Connection.** Activities focused on building relationships (give kudos to another member, ask a question you've been wondering about)

- **Days 15–21: Contribution.** Opportunities to add value (share a resource that's helped you, answer a question in your area of expertise)

- **Days 22–30: Commitment.** Actions that cement community identity (create a small piece of content, commit to a personal next step, reflect on your journey)

The results:

- Participation from members who had been silent for months

- A 347% increase in member-to-member interactions

- Several new collaborations and partnerships that formed between members

- A dramatic shift in culture from consumption to contribution

> **THE MAGIC ELEMENT:** Consistency. By showing up daily with clear, achievable prompts, the community established a new normal of active participation that extended well beyond the thirty-day challenge itself.

THE TECHNOLOGY TANGO

Yes, tools matter. But they're the backdrop, not the main event. Whether you're using Circle, Mighty Networks, Discourse, or another platform, focus on:

- **Making it ridiculously easy for members to find and connect with each other.** Implement clear member directories with searchable skills and interests, and encourage complete profiles with ice-breaker questions.

- **Keeping the user experience clean, intuitive, and friction-free.** Audit your platform regularly from a new member's perspective. Where are they getting stuck? What's confusing? Eliminate unnecessary steps between intent and action.

- **Integrating tools that enhance interaction, and don't add clutter.** Every feature should serve a clear purpose in your engagement strategy. If you can't explain how a tool advances your community's goals, it probably doesn't belong in your stack.

TACKLING THE TOP THREE ENGAGEMENT CHALLENGES

Even the most thoughtfully designed community will face engagement hurdles. Here's how to address the most common challenges:

Challenge one: The crickets problem

You post a thought-provoking question and...silence. Nothing but crickets. I have mentioned crickets before because no reaction to a post can be painful. It is a good idea to think about why you posted; was it to share content? Was it to boost reactions? The why of your post matters and impacts how you are going to feel about reactions or lack of reaction.

SOLUTION: Create momentum with planned participation. Have three to five community members (or team members) ready to jump in with thoughtful responses. Most people don't want to be first, but they'll happily join an existing conversation.

PREVENTATIVE MEASURE: Test your prompts before posting. If you struggle to answer your own question or find it too complex, vague, or time-consuming, your members will too. The best engagement prompts are specific, relatable, and can be answered in under 2 minutes.

Challenge two: The same few voices

Only a small percentage of members actively participate, creating an "insider" dynamic that can alienate others.

SOLUTION: Directly invite quiet members to contribute in low-pressure ways. "Lee, I remember you mentioned experience with email marketing. Would you be willing to share one tip in our discussion this week?"

PREVENTATIVE MEASURE: Create participation formats that explicitly invite different experience levels. "This week we want to hear from members who are just starting out with podcasting. What's one question you have for the group?"

Challenge 3: Surface-level engagement

Lots of activity but little depth—quick likes and generic comments rather than meaningful exchanges.

SOLUTION: Model the depth you want to see by asking thoughtful follow-up questions. "That's fascinating, Dee. Can you share more about how that approach affected your client relationships?"

PREVENTATIVE MEASURE: Create structured formats that guide members toward deeper sharing.

THREE-LAYER SHARE: Tell us 1) what happened, 2) how you felt about it, and 3) what you learned that others might apply.

Remember that engagement isn't an end, it's a means to delivering the transformation your community promises. Every engagement strategy should ultimately connect back to your community's purpose and the value members expect to receive.

PRACTICAL APPLICATION: YOUR NINETY-DAY ENGAGEMENT BLUEPRINT

Ready to put these principles into action? Here's a step-by-step framework for building your engagement strategy.

Phase one: Foundation (days 1–30)

1. **Audit current engagement**

   - Which content and activities generate the most meaningful participation?
   - Who are your most active members, and what motivates them?
   - What barriers might be preventing more widespread engagement?

2. **Design your core rhythm**

   - Establish two to three weekly touchpoints that align with your community's purpose.
   - Create templates for consistent execution.

- Set up a content calendar with themes and prompts.

3. Train your first responders

- Identify five to seven members who can help ensure no post goes unanswered.
- Provide guidelines on creating welcoming, generative responses.
- Recognize their contributions consistently.

Phase two: Expansion (days 31–60)

1. Implement engagement pathways

- Create structured experiences for different member segments.
- Launch your first thirty-day challenge or focused initiative.
- Develop recognition systems for consistent participation.

2. Diversify engagement formats

- Introduce at least three new engagement formats from the list above.
- Collect feedback on which formats resonate most with your members.
- Refine your approach based on actual participation data.

3. Enhance member-to-member connection

- Implement formal or informal matchmaking to connect members.

- Create dedicated spaces for peer support and collaboration.
- Highlight examples of valuable member-to-member interaction.

Phase three: Optimization (days 61–90)

1. Analyze engagement patterns.

- Which formats, times, and topics generate the most meaningful engagement?
- Where in the member journey does participation typically drop off?
- What distinguishes your most engaged members from others?

2. Develop engagement recovery systems.

- Create a reengagement plan for members who have gone quiet.
- Implement "we miss you" outreach with a specific invitation to return.
- Design streamlined ways for lapsed members to rejoin the conversation.

3. Build sustainability

- Document your most effective engagement strategies.
- Train additional members in facilitation and leadership.
- Create systems to maintain engagement when you're not available.

Remember that engagement is iterative. Your strategy should evolve based on what resonates with your specific community. Measure not just the quantity of interactions but also their quality and impact on member satisfaction and outcomes.

MEASURING WHAT MATTERS: BEYOND VANITY METRICS

Not all engagement is created equal. Focus on the metrics that truly indicate community health.

Activity metrics

- **Active member percentage:** What proportion of your total membership participated in the last thirty days?

- **Conversation rate:** How many posts generate actual discussion (multiple responses) versus sitting inactive?

- **Response time:** How quickly do questions or posts receive their first response?

Relationship metrics

- **Member-to-member ratio:** What percentage of interactions happen between members versus between members and moderators?

- **Connection formation:** How many new member-to-member relationships form each month?

- **Collaboration instances:** How often do members work together on projects or support each other's goals?

Impact metrics

- **Transformation stories:** How many members can point to specific positive changes resulting from community participation?

- **Retention rate:** What percentage of members remain active after three, six, and twelve months?

- **Net Promoter Score:** How likely are members to recommend your community to others?

The most revealing question you can ask isn't "How many comments did we get?" but rather "Did this engagement help our members move closer to their goals?"

GUIDING QUESTIONS

1. Think about a time when you were deeply engaged in an online community. What specific experiences or interactions hooked you? How can you re-create that magic for your members?

2. Imagine your community a year from now. What kinds of conversations and connections do you want to see happening? What needs to shift to make that a reality?

3. How can you empower your members to take ownership of engagement? What roles or opportunities could you create for them to step up and lead?

4. What's one engagement format or experience you haven't tried yet that might resonate strongly with your community's needs and interests?

5. How might you better connect your engagement activities to your community's core purpose and the transformation members seek?

PODCAST RECOMMENDATIONS

> **NOTE:** These podcasts were accessible at the time of writing in March 2025. If you aren't finding these specific episodes, please search for similar content in YouTube.

- The Collective Mindset. This podcast is hosted by David DeWald and serves as a "backstage pass to the world of online community management." Each episode features interviews with top community experts who share their strategies for building engaged digital spaces. It's especially recommended for those working in the tech industry as community managers or those aspiring to such roles.

- Get Together. A podcast created and hosted by People & Company, it features interviews with successful community managers, organizers, and creators about their community-building journeys. Hosts Bailey Richardson (who helped shape communities around Instagram and IDEO and cofounded People & Co.) and Kevin Huyhn (fellow P&C cofounder and coauthor of Get Together) explore how these leaders started their communities and what strategies they've developed to unlock growth and engagement. Each episode provides insights into acquiring first members, increasing engagement, and building comprehensive community strategies.

FAQS

1. **I'm struggling with getting members to participate. Should I create more content?**

   More content rarely solves engagement problems. Instead, focus on removing barriers to participation and creating safe spaces for members to connect. Sometimes less is more, try a single, well-facilitated discussion rather than multiple competing threads. Remember that lurking is often the first step toward participation, so make sure your content is valuable even for those who aren't yet ready to contribute.

2. **How do I keep engagement going when I'm not online?**

   Empower your members to lead discussions and create connections. Build a system of volunteer moderators and content creators who are trained in your engagement philosophy. Create scheduling tools and templates that allow you to plan engagement activities in advance. Most important, foster a culture where members feel ownership of the community and naturally step up to maintain its energy.

3. **How much engagement is enough?**

   Focus on quality over quantity. Ten meaningful interactions are worth more than a hundred surface-level comments. Watch for signs of genuine connection, members helping each other, sharing vulnerabilities, celebrating wins together. The right amount of engagement is whatever delivers the transformation your community promises. For some communities, that might mean daily interaction, for others, deeper but less frequent exchanges.

4. **My members say they're too busy to engage. How do I overcome this?**

   Make participation ridiculously easy. Create engagement opportunities that take less than 2 minutes to complete. Be extremely clear about the value members will receive from participating. Consider audio or voice message options for members who can engage while multitasking. Most important, make sure the engagement you're requesting directly connects to the reason they joined your community in the first place.

5. **How do I reactivate a community where engagement has dwindled?**

Start by personally reaching out to previously active members to understand what changed. Relaunch with a focused, time-limited challenge that has clear benefits. Be transparent about your intention to revitalize the community and invite members to shape its new direction. Sometimes a fresh start with a community reset can reignite enthusiasm more effectively than trying to gradually build back momentum.

CHAPTER SUMMARY

Engagement is the lifeblood of any thriving community. But it's not about constant activity or superficial interactions. It's about creating experiences and rituals that foster genuine connection and meaningful participation.

The most effective engagement strategies:

- Are built on a clear understanding of the engagement pyramid - the progression from passive consumption (reading/observing), to interaction (commenting/questioning), to contribution (sharing ideas/resources), and ultimately to creation (initiating projects/leading initiatives).

- Combine the five key ingredients of purpose, safety, social proof, progressive challenge, and recognition.

- Follow a consistent rhythm with daily touchpoints, weekly rituals, and monthly themes.

- Use diverse formats that cater to different participation preferences and community needs.

- Address common challenges proactively with tested solutions.

- Measure what truly matters, the relationships formed and transformations achieved.

By designing an intentional engagement architecture, offering experiences that matter, and empowering your members to take the lead, you create a community that people can't help but want to be a part of.

REMEMBER: You're not just building a platform or creating content; you're designing experiences that change people's lives. Make every interaction count. Create spaces where people feel seen, heard, and valued. That's when true engagement happens.

CHAPTER 5 WORKSHEET

Engagement Architecture: Building Participation That Matters

Ready to create some community magic? Let's design an engagement architecture that'll have your members saying, "I can't imagine not being here!" Fill this out with the same energy you want to see in your community!

SECTION A: LET'S GET THIS PARTY STARTED!

These are all activities to consider. There is no expectation whatsoever that you will select all of them. Safeguard your energy and pick a schedule and activities that nurture you as well as your community. Leverage workflow tools to help you automate and establish repeatable processes.

You're the host of this party, not the entertainment. Your job is to create spaces where others shine.

Engagement pyramid mapping

For each level, identify your current offerings and gaps.

Consumption (reading and viewing)

Current opportunities: _____

Ideas for improvement: _____

Reaction (likes, polls, emojis):

Current opportunities: _____

Ideas for improvement: _____

Contribution (comments and responses):

Current opportunities: _____

Ideas for improvement: _____

Collaboration (working together):

Current opportunities: _____

Ideas for improvement: _____

Creation (member-led initiatives):

Current opportunities: _____

Ideas for improvement: _____

Core engagement types
Map your primary engagement methods.

Learning activities

Format: _____

Frequency: _____

Success measure: _____

Connection opportunities

Format: _____

Frequency: _____

Success measure: _____

Growth experiences

Format: _____

Frequency: _____

Success measure: _____

Engagement-rhythm planning
Create your ideal engagement calendar.

Daily touchpoints

Morning: _____

Midday: _____

Evening: _____

Weekly highlights

Monday: Member spotlights

Content type: _____

Engagement prompt: _____

Follow-up plan: _____

Wednesday: Win celebration

Format: _____

Recognition method: _____

Community involvement: _____

Friday: Community building

Activity type: _____

Participation goal: _____

Success metric: _____

SECTION B: YOUR ENGAGEMENT TOOLKIT
(No boring stuff!)

Format selection and planning

Choose three to five formats to implement in your community. Mix it up to keep things fresh. Nobody wants the "How's everyone doing today?" post for the forty-seventh time.

Hot seat

Implementation approach: _____

Member selection process: _____

Facilitation plan: _____

Peer challenges

Challenge topic: _____

Duration: _____

Support structure: _____

Rapid-fire roundtables

Topic selection: _____

Time constraint: _____

Output creation: _____

Sharing experiences

Prompt development: _____

Safety measures: _____

Connection strategy: _____

Resource exchange

Organization method: _____

Visibility plan: _____

Follow-up system: _____

Celebration rituals

Recognition format: _____

Frequency: _____

Amplification strategy: _____

Expert AMAs (Ask-Me-Anythings)

Expert selection: _____

Preparation process: _____

Content repurposing: _____

Thirty-day challenge design
Create your own engagement challenge.

Week one: Foundation

Day one: _____

Day two: _____

Day three: _____

Day four: _____

Day five: _____

Weekend activity: _____

Week two: Connection

Day eight: _____

Day nine: _____

Day ten: _____

Day eleven: _____

Day twelve: _____

Weekend activity: _____

Week three: Contribution

Day fifteen: _____

Day sixteen: _____

Day seventeen: _____

Day eighteen: _____

Day nineteen: _____

Weekend activity: _____

Week four: Commitment

Day twenty-two: _____

Day twenty-three: _____

Day twenty-four: _____

Day twenty-five: _____

Day twenty-six: _____

Final reflection: _____

SECTION C: CONTENT THAT MAKES PEOPLE SAY, "YES!"

Content mix planning

If your content were a playlist, would people put it on repeat? Plan your greatest hits.

Type	Purpose	Frequency	Platform
Discussion prompts			
Expert Content			
Member Spotlights			
Resource Sharing			
Community Updates			

Content calendar template

Week of: _____

Theme: _____

Goal: _____

	Mon	Tues	Wed	Thur	Fri
Content					
Goal					
Measure					

SECTION D: RESCUING YOUR COMMUNITY FROM THE DREADED CRICKETS

Crickets-problem strategy
Because nothing kills a vibe faster than posting "Anyone here?" to an empty room.

First responders list: _____

Pre-planned seed responses: _____

Prompt testing process: _____

Personal outreach template: _____

Same few voices strategy
Diversifying participation.

Quiet member identification: _____

Direct invitation approach: _____

Recognition for new voices: _____

Segment-specific prompts: _____

Surface-level engagement strategy
Deepening conversation quality.

Follow-up question bank: _____

Depth-encouraging formats: _____

Vulnerability modeling approach: _____

Value-highlighting method: _____

SECTION E: MEASURING THE MAGIC (BEYOND LIKES AND VIEWS)

Success metrics dashboard
Because what gets measured gets celebrated! Track monthly.

Active participation rate: _____

Member-to-member interactions: _____

New relationship formations: _____

Content engagement levels: _____

Event attendance: _____

Response time average: _____

Transformation stories collected: _____

Quality assessment
Rate each engagement type (1–5).

_____ Depth of conversation

_____ Member satisfaction

_____ Value creation

_____ Community building

_____ Knowledge sharing

_____ Relationship formation

_____ Purpose alignment

SECTION F: LEVEL UP YOUR ENGAGEMENT GAME

Current state analysis
Be brutally honest here. Your community deserves your best insights.

What's Working	What's Not	Ideas to Try

Engagement experiments

New Idea	Expected Outcome	Timeline	Measure

SECTION G: CREATING FOMO-WORTHY SPECIAL EVENTS

Quarterly event calendar
Plan experiences so good your members would schedule a vacation for them.

Month one: _____

Event type: _____

Goal: _____

Success measure: _____

Month two: _____

Event type: _____

Goal: _____

Success measure: _____

Month three: _____

Event type: _____

Goal: _____

Success measure: _____

Event success template pre-event:

☐ Goal setting

☐ Promotion plan

☐ Resource preparation

☐ Team assignments

During event:

☐ Engagement tracking

☐ Real-time adjustments

☐ Member support

Post event:

☐ Feedback collection

☐ Success measurement

☐ Follow-up plan

☐ Content repurposing

SECTION H: YOUR NINETY-DAY ROAD MAP TO ENGAGEMENT AWESOMENESS

Phase one: Foundation (days 1–30)

☐ Audit current engagement (the good, the bad, the crickets)

☐ Design your core rhythm (your community's heartbeat)

☐ Train your first responders (your engagement emergency team)

> **YOUR MANTRAS FOR THIS PHASE:** "Test, learn, adjust" and "No post left behind!"

Phase two: Expansion (days 31–60)

☐ Implement engagement pathways (from lurkers to leaders)

☐ Diversify your formats (because variety is the spice of community life)

☐ Enhance member-to-member connection (playing matchmaker)

YOUR MANTRAS FOR THIS PHASE: "Connection over content" and "Make it easy to participate"

Phase three: Optimization (days 61–90)

☐ Analyze patterns (finding your community's unique engagement fingerprint)

☐ Develop recovery systems (bringing the quiet ones back)

☐ Build sustainability (so engagement continues even when you're on a beach somewhere)

YOUR MANTRAS FOR THIS PHASE: "Quality over quantity" and "Systems beat willpower"

CELEBRATION CHECKPOINT!

You've completed this worksheet, which means you're well on your way to creating a community that people can't imagine not being part of! Take a moment to acknowledge your kickass community-building skills.

☐ I'm creating engagement that matters, not just noise.

☐ I'm designing experiences that transform lives, not just pass time.

☐ I'm building a community that feels like home, not just another platform.

Now go implement these ideas and watch your community come alive!

LOOKING AHEAD

Now that you've got your engagement engine humming, it's time to turn our attention to growth. In Chapter 6, we'll explore how to expand your community in a way that deepens connection, rather than dilutes it. We'll explore how to scale these engagement strategies while keeping that intimate, connected feel your members love. Get ready to scale with soul!

SCALING WITH SOUL: GROWING COMMUNITIES THAT THRIVE

"Ignore the nonbelievers. That took away a lot of my energy and attention. Instead, when I started focusing on the people who wanted to engage, things became much better and more elegant."

—S., a humble, engaged Purple Space community member.

In the digital landscape where communities rise and fall daily, one question haunts every successful community builder: "How do I grow without losing what makes us special?" You've built something magical, a space where people feel genuinely connected, where transformation happens, where members can't imagine not being part of it. Now you're facing the exhilarating (and slightly terrifying) challenge of growth.

The good news? Growth doesn't have to mean losing intimacy. The most powerful communities scale by multiplying meaningful experiences, not just adding more members. In this chapter, we'll explore how to grow your community while keeping, and even amplifying, the magic that makes it special.

THE GROWTH PARADOX: BIGGER ISN'T ALWAYS BETTER

In our metric-obsessed world, it's easy to fall into the trap of equating growth with success. "We hit 10,000 members!" sounds impressive until you realize only fifty of them are engaged.

Here's the truth: A community of one hundred deeply engaged members is far more powerful than a community of one thousand disengaged ones. Much like the song from Dear Evan Hansen, "You will be found."

As Jono Bacon puts it: "Communities are not channels or platforms. They are shared purpose and shared value creation." This insight strikes at the core of what it means to scale a community with soul. It's not about chasing vanity metrics or exponential growth at all costs. It's about staying true to your purpose, deepening connections, and creating value at every stage of your community's journey.

In our increasingly digital world, genuine connection has become more valuable than ever. The ability to create real, meaningful relationships online isn't just nice to have, it's a superpower. As Keith, one of Purple Space's highly engaged members, beautifully expresses: "It's something integral to our humanness; we want connection. The future isn't about the platforms we use but the spaces we create within them."

THREE MODELS OF COMMUNITY SCALING

Before we dive into tactics, let's understand the three fundamental ways communities can scale and which ways might be right for yours.

1. Depth scaling: Growing impact, not size

In this model, you deliberately keep your community small (typically under 200 members) while continuously deepening the value, connection, and transformation members experience.

Signs this might be right for you:

- Your community thrives on high-touch, personalized experiences.

- Members value exclusivity and intimate connections.

- Your business model supports higher member fees for premium experiences.

- You enjoy knowing each member personally.

> **EXAMPLE:** A mastermind community for executive women might cap membership at 150 but continuously enhance the depth of connections, resources, and transformational experiences available.

2. Segment scaling: Growing through specialization

In this model, you create distinct subcommunities or cohorts organized around specific interests, goals, or demographic factors, each with its own leadership and culture within your broader community ecosystem.

Signs this might be right for you:

- Your community attracts members with diverse but related interests.

- Members have expressed a desire for more specialized connections.

- You have potential leaders who could own specific segments.

- Your purpose supports multiple pathways to transformation.

  EXAMPLE: A community for creative entrepreneurs might develop specialized segments for writers, designers, coaches, and course creators, each with dedicated spaces and programming.

3. Structure scaling: Growing through systems

In this model, you build robust systems, processes, and leadership structures that allow your community to grow while maintaining a consistent culture and quality of experience.

Signs this might be right for you:

- Your community serves a broad audience with a universal need.

- You have a strong, well-defined culture that can be systematized.

- You're willing to invest in technology and team development.

- Your purpose benefits from reaching more people.

  EXAMPLE: A community for first-time parents might grow to thousands of members by developing clear onboarding paths, training volunteer moderators, and creating systematic touchpoints for support.

Most thriving communities eventually use elements from all three models, but understanding your primary scaling approach will help you make strategic decisions as you grow.

FIVE PILLARS OF SCALING WITH SOUL

No matter which scaling model resonates most with your community vision, the architecture that these five pillars govern will help you grow without losing your soul.

Pillar one: Purpose-aligned growth strategy

Growing without purpose is like building a house without a foundation, it might look impressive initially, but it won't stand the test of time.

Key actions:

- Revisit your community purpose statement regularly as you grow. Does it still capture the transformation you provide? Is it clear enough to guide your scaling decisions?

- Create a "Not For Us" list that explicitly states who your community isn't designed to serve and what values don't align with your culture. This clarity helps you say no to growth opportunities that would dilute your community's essence.

- Develop growth metrics that reflect impact, not just size. Instead of the number of new members, track the number of transformation stories or the percentage of members who've achieved their primary goal.

Community growth expert Sarah Hawk notes: "The most successful communities aren't trying to be everything to everyone. They're laser-focused on delivering extraordinary value to a specific group of people in a way that aligns perfectly with their purpose."

Pillar two: Intentional onboarding at scale

As you grow, your onboarding process becomes even more critical. It's no longer just about welcoming new members; it's about transferring your community's DNA.

Key actions:

- Design a multi-touchpoint onboarding journey that gradually introduces new members to your community's purpose, culture, and opportunities for connection. This might include welcome videos, orientation calls, buddy systems, and graduated engagement activities.

- Create a Community Compass document that captures your community's essential elements: purpose, values, norms, rituals, and pathways to participation. This becomes your North Star as you scale.

- Build feedback loops into onboarding to continuously improve the experience. Regular surveys, interviews with new members, and monitoring early engagement patterns help you refine your approach.

Pillar three: Microcommunities and connection architecture

As your community grows, creating structures for meaningful connection becomes essential. Without intentional design, larger communities can feel overwhelming and impersonal.

Key actions:

- Implement the 7-70-700 framework: Design experiences for intimate groups of seven, medium-sized groups of around seventy, and a full community of hundreds or thousands. Each size serves different connection needs.

- Create "neighborhoods" within your community based on shared interests, experience levels, goals, or geographic location. These microcommunities create the feeling of a small town, even as your overall community grows.

- Develop progression pathways that move members from general community participation to more intimate micro-community experiences as they demonstrate engagement and alignment.

Research on optimal group sizes supports this approach. The Dunbar number theory suggests humans can maintain stable, meaningful relationships with about 150 people, and with closer circles of approximately fifty, fifteen, and five people for increasingly intimate connections. Your community architecture should reflect these natural human grouping tendencies.

Implementation spotlight: Scaling through cohorts

One powerful scaling approach is the cohort model, where members progress through experiences together in groups of twenty to fifty people. Here's how to implement it:

1. ***Define the cohort journey:*** Create a clear pathway with beginning, middle, and end points.

2. ***Balance structure with organic connection:*** Provide enough structure to create a shared experience but enough freedom for authentic relationships to form.

3. ***Train cohort facilitators:*** Develop clear guidelines and training for those leading each cohort.

4. ***Plan for cohort graduation:*** Design how cohort members will transition into the broader community or advanced experiences.

Cohorts create a sense of belonging and shared journey that can persist even as your overall community grows to hundreds or thousands.

Pillar four: Distributed leadership model

As your community scales, trying to do everything yourself becomes impossible. The key to sustainable growth is empowering members to take on meaningful leadership roles.

Key actions:

- Map leadership roles and responsibilities that distribute ownership across your community. These might include content creators, welcome ambassadors, event hosts, technical support, and microcommunity leaders.

- Create a leadership development pipeline that identifies potential leaders, provides training and mentorship, offers graduated responsibilities, and celebrates leadership contributions.

- Establish clear leadership principles and guidelines that ensure consistency while allowing for individual expression and innovation.

Richard Millington observes that "the most successful communities at scale aren't led by a single charismatic figure, but by a diverse network of empowered members who each own a piece of the community's success."

Pillar five: Scalable systems and rituals

The final pillar of scaling with soul is creating systems and rituals that can grow with your community while maintaining their meaning and impact.

Key actions:

- Document core processes for everything from content creation to conflict resolution. These playbooks ensure consistency and quality as new leaders emerge.

- Design scalable versions of your community rituals. For example, a welcome ritual might evolve from the founder personally greeting each new member to a structured welcome thread where established members each greet one newcomer.

- Implement technology that supports connection at scale. Choose platforms and tools that make it easy for members to find relevant content, connect with each other, and participate in ways that align with their preferences.

As David Spinks notes: "Culture is the single most important factor in a community's success." Your systems and rituals are the vehicles through which your culture reproduces itself as you scale.

THE FOUR STAGES OF COMMUNITY GROWTH

Understanding where your community is in its growth journey helps you focus on the right scaling strategies at the right time. Here's a framework for navigating the four common growth stages:

Stage one: Foundation (0–100 members)

Focus areas

- Establishing core purpose and values
- Creating initial rituals and traditions
- Building a strong sense of belonging
- Gathering stories of transformation

A scaling trap to avoid. It is counterproductive to try and grow too quickly before your foundation is solid. A rushed foundation leads to a fragile community.

Stage two: Expansion (100–500 members)

Focus areas

- Implementing your first microcommunities
- Identifying and developing initial leaders among the members
- Creating more structured onboarding
- Systematizing key community processes

A scaling trap to avoid: Avoid diluting your community's purpose to attract more members. Stay true to who you are and what makes your community special.

Stage three: Organization (500–1,000+ members)

Focus areas

- Developing robust leadership structures

- Creating connection pathways between microcommunities

- Implementing more sophisticated technology solutions

- Building stronger feedback and adaptation systems

A scaling trap to avoid. Try not to become overly rigid in your systems, which could lead to losing the heart of your community. Systems should serve connection, not replace it.

Stage four: Evolution (1,000+ members)

Focus areas

- Innovating new member experiences

- Creating leadership transition processes

- Developing sustainability models (financial and operational)

- Measuring and amplifying community impact

A scaling trap to avoid. Make every effort not to lose touch with your community's front lines. Create systems to stay connected to member experiences and emerging needs.

CASE STUDY: SCALING WITH HEART

Nicole Russo, founder of the I Heart My Life community, was clear that she wanted to grow her community without losing the magic. Here's how she did it.

1. *Clarity of purpose:* From day one, Nicole was clear that her community was about helping women build businesses and

lives they love. Every decision she made, from the content she created to the partners she chose, led up to that purpose.

2. *Culture of celebration:* Nicole made celebration a core part of her community's culture. She regularly spotlighted member wins, hosted virtual dance parties, and created a Wall of Love, where members could share gratitude for each other. As the community grew, these rituals scaled with it.

3. *Micro-masterminds:* As her community approached 1,000 members, Nicole introduced micro-mastermind groups, where members could connect around specific goals and challenges. These groups created pockets of intimacy and accountability within the larger community.

4. *Empowered leadership:* Nicole identified members who embodied her community's values and empowered them to lead. Some hosted local meetups, others moderated discussions, and a few even created their own courses. This distributed leadership allowed the community to scale without losing its heart.

The result? A community that grew to over 20,000 members while maintaining its soul. Members consistently report that despite its size, I Heart My Life still feels intimate, supportive, and aligned with its original vision.

GROWTH AND MONETIZATION: THE DELICATE BALANCE

As your community scales, the question of monetization naturally arises. How do you generate sustainable revenue without compromising the connection that makes your community valuable? This balance becomes even more critical as you grow.

There are two very different foundational perspectives. Each approach has its own key principles: One perspective is to demonstrate your community's value first, followed by monetization. The other approach is to always have a paywall because people pay attention to and tend to value what they pay for.

First, understand your own strategy and build with that intention in mind.

- **Value first, monetization second:** Always lead with exceptional value that aligns with your community's purpose. When members experience genuine transformation, they're happy to invest in deepening that experience.

- **Multiple revenue streams:** Develop diverse income sources that serve different member needs and price points. This might include core membership fees, premium experiences, digital products, affiliate partnerships, or sponsored content.

- **Transparent value exchange:** Be crystal clear about what members receive in exchange for their investment. Avoid hidden fees or unclear value propositions that erode trust.

- **Community-centric approach:** Involve your members in monetization decisions. Seek their input on what additional experiences or resources they would value enough to pay for.

MONETIZATION SPOTLIGHT: TIERED-MEMBERSHIP MODEL

One effective approach for growing communities is implementing a tiered-membership structure along the following options.

Free tier: Provides a taste of your community's value with limited access to content and experiences.

Core membership: Offers full access to the community, regular events, and foundational resources.

Premium tier: Adds exclusive experiences, deeper support, and advanced resources.

High-touch tier: Provides personalized guidance, smaller group experiences, and direct access to leadership.

This model allows members to self-select the level of investment and experience that matches their needs and capacity, while providing multiple revenue streams to support your community's growth.

We'll dive deeper into monetization strategies in Chapter 7 and remember: Your approach to revenue should always reinforce, not undermine, the connection that makes your community valuable in the first place. Let's return to our discussion about scaling with soul.

As Eva Forde, notes, "…community is fundamental to me, my mental health, my well-being…We are social beings," she says, "not every community is created equal and so not every community is good for my well-being." As community leaders, it's our responsibility to foster cultures and provide guidelines that keep our members safe and thriving, even as we grow.

PRACTICAL APPLICATION: YOUR SCALING BLUEPRINT

Ready to scale with soul? Here's a step-by-step approach to growing your community while preserving its magic.

Step one: Assess your current state.

Before mapping your growth strategy, honestly evaluate where your community stands now:

- How strong is your current foundation of purpose, culture, and engagement?

- What elements of your community experience are most valued by members?

- Where are the friction points that might become problematic at a larger scale?

- Which of the three scaling models (depth, segment, or structure) resonates most with your vision?

Step 2: Design your scaling architecture.

Based on your assessment, create the frameworks that will support healthy growth.

- Document your community DNA (purpose, values, culture, and key experiences).

- Map your microcommunity structure and connection pathways.

- Design your leadership development and distribution model.

- Create scalable versions of your core rituals and traditions.

Step 3: Implement growth systems.

With your architecture in place, focus on the systems that will facilitate smooth scaling.

- Develop your enhanced onboarding journey.

- Create playbooks for key community processes.

- Implement technology solutions that support your growth model.

- Establish feedback loops to monitor community health during growth.

Step 4: Activate strategic growth.

Now you're ready to actively grow your community with intention. So:

- Launch your member referral program.

- Implement your content and social media strategy.

- Initiate partnerships with aligned communities or influencers.

- Host strategic public events that showcase your community's value.

Step 5: Adapt and evolve.

As you grow, continuously refine your approach based on feedback and results like these:

- Monitor key metrics for community health and member satisfaction.

- Regularly gather qualitative feedback through surveys and conversations.

- Make iterative improvements to your scaling systems.

- Stay connected to your community's evolving needs and aspirations.

Remember that scaling with soul is not a linear process but a continuous cycle of intentional growth, listening, adapting, and refining. The communities that thrive at scale are those that remain profoundly connected to their purpose while being willing to evolve how they deliver on that purpose.

MEASURING SCALING SUCCESS

As you scale, it's important to track metrics that align with your community's purpose and values. Some key ones to consider:

- Member engagement depth (quality and frequency of participation)
- Relationship formation rate (new connections between members)
- Microcommunity health (engagement within smaller groups)
- Leadership emergence (number and impact of member leaders)
- Purpose alignment (how well activity connects to community purpose)
- Transformation stories (documented member outcomes)
- Retention by cohort (how long members from each growth phase stay)

Remember, these metrics are a means to an end, creating a thriving, impactful community. Don't get so caught up in the numbers that you lose sight of the human beings behind them.

GUIDING QUESTIONS

1. What unique aspects of your community's culture must be preserved as you scale? How will you ensure these elements remain central to the member experience?

2. How will you structure your community to maintain intimate connections even as you grow? Which microcommunity model most resonates with your vision?

3. What leadership qualities are most important for your community? How will you identify and develop members who embody these qualities?

4. What systems or processes in your community would break under the pressure of growth? How can you redesign them to be more scalable?

How will you measure whether you're scaling with soul? What indicators would show you're growing without losing your community's essence?

PODCAST RECOMMENDATIONS

NOTE: These podcasts were accessible at the time of writing in March 2025.

- For a deeper dive into scaling with soul, check out the Masters of Community podcast episode with Scott Guthrie on "Growing communities with compassion." Scott shares powerful insights on how to scale while staying true to your community's core values.

- Also worth exploring is the Community Corner podcast episode featuring Carrie Melissa Jones discussing "The Architecture of Belonging at Scale." Her framework for creating connection pathways in larger communities offers practical wisdom for growth-minded community builders.

FAQS

1. **How do you maintain intimacy as the community grows?**

   Scale through multiplication, not addition. Create subgroups, empower member leaders, and maintain consistent small-group experiences. As Saurabh advises, focus on the people who want to engage rather than trying to connect with everyone at once. Remember that intimacy happens between members, not just between members and founders.

2. **What's the ideal group size for meaningful connection?**

   Research shows that groups of four to eight people typically foster the best connections. For intimate discussions, aim for three to four people. For collaborative projects, five to eight works well. Larger groups should be broken down into smaller units for deeper connection. Design your community architecture with these natural human grouping tendencies in mind.

3. **How quickly should we grow our community?**

   There's no universal right pace, it depends on your community's purpose, resources, and readiness. Generally, it's better to grow more slowly than you think you should. Adding members faster than your culture and systems can integrate them typically leads to diluted experience and higher churn. Focus on graduating through the growth stages with a solid foundation at each level.

4. **When should we start implementing a distributed leadership model?**

   Start identifying and nurturing potential leaders from day one, even in a small community. Begin with simple leadership opportunities (hosting a thread, welcoming new members) and gradually increase responsibility as your community grows. By the time you reach 100 to 200 members, you should have a defined leadership structure with multiple members taking ownership of community aspects.

5. **How do we balance monetization with maintaining our community's soul?**

   Always lead with value and align monetization with your community's purpose. Involve members in monetization decisions by seeking their input on what additional experiences they'd value enough to pay for. Create diverse revenue streams that serve different member needs and price points. Remember that members are happy to invest in experiences that deliver real transformation.

CHAPTER SUMMARY

Scaling with soul is about growing your community in a way that deepens connection, rather than dilutes it. By understanding the three models of community scaling—depth, segment, and structure—you can choose the approach that best aligns with your vision.

The five pillars of scaling with soul provide a comprehensive framework for growth. They include:

1. Purpose-aligned growth strategy

2. Intentional onboarding at scale

3. Microcommunities and connection architecture

4. Distributed leadership model

5. Scalable systems and rituals

As your community progresses through the four growth stages— foundation, expansion, organization, and evolution—you'll face different challenges and opportunities. By focusing on the right priorities at each stage and avoiding common scaling traps, you can grow while preserving the magic that makes your community special.

Remember that scaling and monetization are intricately connected. In our next chapter, we'll dive deeper into creating sustainable revenue models that support your community's growth while enhancing, not undermining, the value you provide to members. Get ready to explore how to measure what matters and monetize in alignment with your community's soul!

CHAPTER 6 WORKSHEET

Scaling with Soul: Growing Communities That Thrive

Ready to grow your community without losing its magic? This worksheet will help you scale with intention and heart. Remember: Bigger isn't always better, but better is always possible.

SECTION A: YOUR SCALING COMPASS

Growth model assessment
Which scaling approach resonates most with your vision? Rate each 1–5 (5 being most aligned):

_____ **Depth scaling:** Growing impact while keeping membership small and exclusive

_____ **Segment scaling:** Creating specialized subcommunities for different member groups

_____ **Structure scaling:** Building systems that support larger membership numbers

Based on these ratings, my primary scaling approach will be:

_____

Because: _____

Community Growth Stage
Check your current stage and focus areas:

Foundation Stage (0–100 members)

My priorities: _____

Core challenges: _____

Success indicators: _____

Expansion Stage (100–500 members)

My priorities: _____

Core challenges: _____

Success indicators: _____

Organization Stage (500–1,000+ members)

My priorities: _____

Core challenges: _____

Success indicators: _____

Evolution Stage (1,000+ members)

My priorities: _____

Core challenges: _____

Success indicators: _____

Soul-Preserving Boundaries
What aspects of your community must be protected as you grow?

Nonnegotiable values: _____

Key member experiences: _____

Cultural elements to preserve: _____

Types of growth to avoid: _____

> **REMEMBER:** What you say no to defines your community as much as what you say yes to.

SECTION B: YOUR CONNECTION ARCHITECTURE

Microcommunity design
How will you create "neighborhoods" within your growing community?

Small Groups (4–8 people):

Format: _____

Formation criteria: _____

Connection frequency: _____

Success measures: _____

Medium Groups (15–50 people):

Format: _____

Organization Method: _____

Leadership approach: _____

Success measures: _____

Large Community (Everyone):

Unifying experiences: _____

All-community rhythm: _____

Cross-group pollination: _____

Success measures: _____

> **PRO TIP:** Design for the human brain! We naturally connect in groups of about five, fifteen, fifty, and one hundred and fifty people. Work with biology, not against it.

Cohort System Planning

Cohort Journey
If using a cohort model for scaling, it's a Cohort Journey

Duration: _____

Key milestones: _____

Graduation criteria: _____

Cohort Structure

Size target: _____

Formation frequency: _____

Leadership model: _____

Connection Rituals

First-day experience: _____

Regular touchpoints: _____

Celebration moments: _____

SECTION C: DISTRIBUTED LEADERSHIP BLUEPRINT

Leadership roles mapping

Identify roles needed as you scale. No superhero capes required! The best communities distribute leadership among many members.

Role	Responsibilities	Skills Needed	Potential Leaders

Leadership development pathway

How will you grow more leaders?

Stage one: Identification

Behaviors to look for: _____

Opportunities to test: _____

Stage two: Cultivation

Training methods: _____

Mentorship approach: _____

Stage three: Empowerment

Responsibility scope: _____

Decision-making authority: _____

Stage four: Recognition

Acknowledgment forms: _____

Rewards and perks: _____

Leadership principles
What guidelines will ensure consistent leadership as you scale?

_____

_____

_____

_____

_____

_____

_____

_____

SECTION D: SCALABLE SYSTEMS DESIGN

Process Documentation
Which core processes need standardization as you grow?

Process	Current Approach	Scalable Version	Documentation Plan
Onboarding			
Content creation			
Event management			
Conflict resolution			
Member recognition			

You are now creating your community operating system! Make it robust but flexible.

Scaling your rituals

How will your key community rituals evolve? Great rituals create the same feeling, regardless of size.

Ritual	Small Version	Medium Version	Large Version

Technology Infrastructure

What tools will support your growth?

Member management

Current solution: _____

Scaling needs: _____

Potential upgrades: _____

Communication channels

Current solution: _____

Scaling needs: _____

Potential upgrades: _____

Content organization

Current solution: _____

Scaling needs: _____

Potential upgrades: _____

Analytics and measurement

Current solution: _____

Scaling needs: _____

Potential upgrades: _____

SECTION E: GROWTH AND MONETIZATION ALIGNMENT

Value Ladder Creation
Design your tiered offering structure. Your pricing should reflect the transformation, not just the features.

Free or entry level

Value provided: _____

Limitations: _____

Growth pathway: _____

Core membership

Value provided: _____

Price point: _____

Key differentiators: _____

Premium experience

Value provided: _____

Price point: _____

Exclusivity factors: _____

High-touch option

Value provided: _____

Price point: _____

Capacity limits: _____

Revenue diversification
Explore multiple streams to support your growth.

Membership fees: _____

Premium experiences: _____

Digital products: _____

Events: _____

Affiliate partnerships: _____

Sponsorships: _____

Other: _____

SECTION F: YOUR NINETY-DAY SCALING PLAN

Break down your scaling journey into manageable phases.

Month 1: Foundation Strengthening

Week 1: _____

Week 2: _____

Week 3: _____

Week 4: _____

Month 2: System Implementation

Week 1: _____

Week 2: _____

Week 3: _____

Week 4: _____

Month 3: Growth Activation

Week 1: _____

Week 2: _____

Week 3: _____

Week 4: _____

Celebratory check-in!

You've mapped out a thoughtful scaling strategy that preserves what makes your community special. That's something to celebrate! Check off your achievements:

☐ I'm committed to growing with intention, not just adding members.

☐ I've designed connection pathways that will work at any size.

☐ I'm building systems that support scale without sacrificing soul.

☐ I've aligned my monetization approach with my community's values.

LOOKING AHEAD

Now that you've designed a growth strategy that preserves your community's soul while expanding its reach, it's time to tackle the question that keeps many community builders up at night: "How do I make this financially sustainable?"

As your community scales, so do your expenses and the time investment required to maintain quality experiences. The passion that fueled your early days isn't enough to sustain your community in the long term—you need a practical economic engine that powers your vision while honoring the connection at its heart.

In Chapter 7, we'll dive deep into monetization models that work for communities, in other words, approaches that enhance rather than detract from the member experience. You'll discover how to:

• Design multiple revenue streams that align with your community's purpose.

- Create pricing structures that reflect the true value you provide.

- Measure what matters beyond dollars and cents.

- Make financial decisions that strengthen rather than compromise your community's soul.

As Richard Millington wisely notes, "The most sustainable communities aren't those with the most features or the cheapest price. They're the ones that deliver the most value relative to their cost." You've built something of tremendous value, now it's time to ensure that value is recognized, rewarded, and able to thrive for the long haul.

Let's next explore how to build a sustainable economic foundation for the vibrant, soul-centered community you've worked so hard to create. After all, a community that can sustain itself financially can continue transforming lives for years to come.

Ready to take your community engagement to the next level? Let's connect on LinkedIn and build something extraordinary together.

CHAPTER 7

MINDFUL MONETIZATION AND MEASUREMENTS

"Your pricing should mirror the transformation you deliver, not just features you provide."

—Keith Hawk, community strategist

L et's talk about the elephant in the community room—monetization. While we're creating value, we also need to foster sustainability, and, as we know, sustainable communities require financial fuel. But how do you fund a mission without compromising its soul? The answer lies in what community expert Jono Bacon calls "value exchange architecture."

THE MONEY MINDSET SHIFT

I get it. You've built this amazing space where people connect, learn, and grow together. The thought of introducing money into this beautiful ecosystem might feel uncomfortable, like you're somehow compromising the magic you've worked so hard to create.

But here's a liberating truth: Sustainable communities need financial fuel.

When done with intention and care, monetization doesn't diminish your community's spirit. It amplifies it. It transforms casual participation into committed investment. It gives you the resources to build something that lasts longer than your enthusiasm (or savings account).

As community expert Jono Bacon puts it: "Communities are not channels or platforms. They are shared purpose and shared value creation." This insight becomes your North Star for ethical, effective monetization.

The transformation equation

Here's a perspective shift that changed everything for me: **People don't pay just for community access; they pay for the transformation it will bring.**

Let that illuminate your thinking for a moment.

When someone buys a gym membership, they're not paying for access to treadmills. They're investing in becoming healthier, stronger, and more confident. Your community is no different. You're not selling entry to a digital space; you're offering a pathway to meaningful change.

Consider these real-world examples:

- Sara's writing community saw a 40% upgrade to paid tiers when she stopped marketing "access to workshops" and started promising "become a published author in ninety days."

- The Freelancer's Hub achieved 80% retention through tiered-value offerings focused on concrete outcomes like "land your first $5K client."

Once you embrace this perspective, your entire approach to monetization shifts. You stop asking, "How much can I charge?" and start asking, "What transformation can I provide?"

BUILDING YOUR VALUE EXCHANGE ARCHITECTURE

Now let's get practical. How do you structure monetization that feels aligned with your values **and** delivers massive value to your members?

Step 1: Map your transformation journey

Before setting prices, get crystal clear on the journey your members take:

1. **Starting point:** What specific challenge or aspiration brings people to your community?

2. **Transformation process:** What key milestones do they experience within your community?

3. **End state:** What measurable outcome do they achieve?

For example:

- **Starting point:** Freelance writers struggling to find consistent clients.

- **Transformation process:** Learning to identify niches, create compelling portfolios, price services, and negotiate contracts.

- **End state:** Booking $5,000-plus per month in recurring client work.

This isn't just a conceptual exercise; it's the blueprint for your entire monetization strategy.

Step 2: Create your value ladder

Every thriving community needs multiple entry points for different commitment levels:

Foundation tier (free)

- **Offer:** Immediate problem-solving tools

- **Example:** Weekly writing prompts and a peer-feedback forum

- **Success metric:** A 70% return rate within thirty days

Core membership ($15–$50/month)

- **Offer:** Guided transformation and community support

- **Example:** Monthly workshops and accountability groups, plus expert feedback

- **Success metric:** Half the members achieving defined outcomes within ninety days

Premium tier ($100–$500/month or one-time high-ticket offers)

- **Offer:** Accelerated results and high-touch support

- **Example:** One-to-one coaching and mastermind groups, plus in-person events

- **Success metric:** A 90% success rate with testimonials that sell your program for you

  PRO TIP: According to Mighty Networks founder Gina Bianchini, the sweet spot for monthly community membership is around $47. But remember, your pricing should reflect the value of transformation, not necessarily industry averages.

REAL-WORLD EXAMPLE: THE TRANSFORMATION-BASED PRICING MODEL

Let me share how this works in practice.

Sara started a community for freelance writers. Initially, she offered everything for free, including weekly prompts, feedback threads, and Q&A sessions. Her community grew quickly, but Sara was pouring in hours each week without sustainable income.

Then she made a thoughtful shift: She mapped her transformation journey and created a three-tier system:

- **Free tier:** Basic writing resources and community forum

- **Core membership ($20/month):** Weekly workshops, personalized feedback, and accountability pods

- **VIP tier ($200/month):** One-to-one coaching, pitch reviews, and client-matching service

The results? Not only did 35% of her free members upgrade, but engagement and success stories flourished. Members weren't just paying for access; they were investing in becoming better, more successful writers.

MONETIZATION MODELS THAT WORK

Let's explore the most effective models for community monetization:

Subscription-based models

- **Best for:** Communities offering ongoing value and continuous support

- **Pricing benchmark:** $15–$50/month for core membership

- **Example:** A wellness community charging $47/month for daily meditation sessions, weekly live classes, and a private forum

> **PRO TIP:** Focus on retention by delivering consistent value that members can't find elsewhere.

Freemium models

- **Best for:** Growing your audience while monetizing the most engaged members

- **Structure:** Free tier with basic resources, plus paid tier with premium offerings

- **Example:** A productivity community offering free time-management tips and a public discussion board, with a $29/month tier for advanced courses and personalized plans.

> **PRO TIP:** Your free tier should be valuable enough to attract members but limited enough to make the paid tier compelling.

> **NOTE:** Be aware: This version can allow spammers and others who are not your Ideal Member to very easily join. You will need to carefully monitor adherence to your community guidelines if you choose this model.

One-time payments

- **Best for:** Stand-alone experiences or resources with clear beginning and end points

- **Structure:** Events, workshops, courses, or digital products

- **Example:** A writing community hosting a $150 weekend virtual retreat with live workshops and a workbook.

   PRO TIP: Use one-time offerings to generate cash flow while building your subscription model

Hybrid Models

- **Best for:** Communities with diverse member needs and varying levels of commitment

- **Structure:** Combination of subscriptions, one-time payments, and premium offerings

- **Example:** A business community with a free tier, a $47/month subscription, and a $500 master class

   PRO TIP: Create clear pathways between offerings to guide members toward deeper engagement

THE PSYCHOLOGY OF PRICING: MAKE YOUR OFFERS IRRESISTIBLE

Pricing isn't just about numbers; it's also about perception. Here's how to position your offerings for maximum perceived value:

1. **Anchor your value**

   - Don't just list features; quantify the transformation.

   - **Example:** "Join our $20/month membership and land your first client within thirty days." (versus "Get access to our job board").

2. **Use strategic price points**

   - Prices ending in seven or nine convert better than round numbers.

   - **Example:** $47/month feels more strategic than $50/month.

3. **Create package comparisons**

   - Show the value by comparing what they get versus what they pay.

   - **Example:** Get $500 plus resources and support for just $47/month.

4. **Offer easy entry points**

   - Remove barriers with trial periods or money-back guarantees

   - **Example:** "Try for seven days, then decide if we're worth it"

PRO TIP: Always be transparent about your pricing. Hidden fees or unexpected costs will erode trust faster than anything else.

MEASURING WHAT MATTERS: THE FRAMEWORK FOR SUCCESS METRICS

Monetization without measurement is like navigating without a compass. You need to track the right metrics to know if your strategy is working.

The seven key metrics every community builder must track

1. Engagement rate

- **Formula:** (Active members ÷ total members) × 100
- **Benchmark:** 30% or more for a healthy community
- **Action step:** If below 20%, audit your content and interaction opportunities.

2. Conversion rate

- **Formula:** (Paid members ÷ free members who explored paid options) × 100
- **Benchmark:** 5%-10% for well-positioned offerings
- **Action step:** If below 3%, revisit your value proposition and pricing strategy.

3. Retention rate

- **Formula:** (Members who renew ÷ total members up for renewal) × 100
- **Benchmark:** 70%+ for sustainable communities
- **Action step:** If below 60%, implement exit surveys and retention campaigns.

4. *Member lifetime value (MLV)*

- **Formula:** Average monthly revenue per member × average membership duration (months)
- **Benchmark:** Varies widely, but aim for 12 × your monthly fee.
- **Action step:** Focus on increasing duration through deeper engagement.

5. *Cost per acquisition (CPA)*

- **Formula:** Total marketing costs ÷ number of new members
- **Benchmark:** Should be less than 30% of your MLV
- **Action step:** Test different acquisition channels to lower your CPA.

6. *Net Promoter Score (NPS)*

- **Formula:** % promoters (9–10 scores) – % detractors (0–.6 scores)
- **Benchmark:** Typically, 30+ is good; 50+ is excellent.
- **Action step:** Survey quarterly and address feedback promptly

7. *Transformation rate*

- **Formula:** (Members achieving stated outcomes ÷ total active members) × 100
- **Benchmark:** More than half of members support transformation-focused communities
- **Action step:** Document and showcase success stories to attract new members.

> **PRO TIP:** Create a monthly dashboard with these metrics. Whatever gets measured gets managed and improved.

AVOIDING THE FIVE COMMON MONETIZATION MISTAKES

Learn from the mistakes of others so you can create a smoother path.

Mistake one: Charging before delivering value

- **The challenge:** Launching paid tiers without proving your community's worth
- **The solution:** Build a thriving free tier first, then introduce paid offerings based on member needs.

Mistake two: Pricing based on your comfort level (not value)

- **The challenge:** Undercharging because monetization feels uncomfortable
- **The solution:** Price based on the transformation you deliver, not your comfort zone

Mistake three: Creating too many options

- **The challenge:** Confusing members with too many packages and pricing tiers
- **The solution:** Limit to three tiers maximum, with clear differentiation between each

Mistake four: Neglecting your free members

- **The challenge:** Focusing exclusively on paid members, once monetization begins

- **The solution:** Continue delivering value to free members; they're your future paid members.

Mistake five: Not evolving your offerings

- **The challenge:** Keeping the same pricing and structure as your community grows

- **The solution:** Regularly review your offerings and increase value (and prices) as your expertise grows.

YOUR THIRTY-DAY MONETIZATION ACTION PLAN

Let's turn all this guidance into action with a step-by-step plan:

Week 1: Map your transformation.

- **Day 1–3:** Document your community's starting point, process, and end state.

- **Day 4–7:** Survey current members about their goals and challenges.

Week 2: Design your value ladder.

- **Day 8–10:** Create your free, core, and premium tier offerings.

- **Day 11–14:** Set strategic pricing based on transformation value.

Week 3: Build your measurement system.

- Day 15–17: Set up tracking for the seven key metrics.
- Day 18–21: Create a monthly dashboard template.

Week 4: Launch and optimize.

- Day 22–25: Introduce your monetization model to your community.
- Day 26–30: Gather initial feedback and make necessary adjustments.

  REMEMBER: Monetization is an iterative process. Start small, measure what matters, and grow with intention.

GUIDING QUESTIONS

1. What specific transformation does your community provide that members can't easily get elsewhere?

2. If your ideal member joined today, what measurable outcome would they achieve within ninety days?

3. What are the top three concerns members might have about paying for your community, and how can you address them thoughtfully?

4. How can you structure your free tier to deliver immediate value while naturally leading members toward paid offerings?

5. Which of the seven key metrics do you need to start tracking immediately to gauge your community's health?

PODCAST RECOMMENDATION

NOTE: This podcast was accessible at the time of writing in March 2025.

- The Community Experience podcast: "Find your people and build an intentional community," with Jillian Benbow and Tony Bacigalupo. The hosts break down ethical monetization strategies that strengthen rather than exploit community bonds.

FAQS

1. **When is the right time to start monetizing my community?**

The best time to introduce monetization is when you have: 1) Consistent engagement from at least one hundred active members, 2) clear evidence that your community delivers tangible value, and 3) multiple requests for more in-depth resources or support. Don't wait for the perfect moment; aim for "ready enough."

2. **How do I transition from free to paid without losing members?**

Communicate the transition early and often, emphasizing the increased value and continued free options. Offer founding-member rates to existing members, and consider a grace period that allows members to experience the new paid features before deciding. Most important, make sure the paid tier delivers significantly more value than the free tier.

3. **What if my members express concerns about pricing?**

Some feedback is normal. Listen to concerns with openness, but don't automatically lower your prices. Instead, focus on more effectively communicating the transformation you provide. If multiple members mention the same concern, consider adjusting your offer structure (not necessarily your price) to better address their needs.

4. **How do I balance monetization with accessibility?**

Create multiple entry points at different price points, offer scholarships or sliding-scale options for those with financial constraints, and maintain a valuable free tier. Remember that sustainability enables you to serve more people over the long term, you can help more people when your community is financially healthy.

5. **How often should I update my pricing?**

Review your pricing every six to twelve months, or whenever you significantly enhance your offerings. As your expertise grows and your community delivers more value, your pricing should reflect that growth. Consider grandfathering existing members at lower rates when you increase prices for new members.

CHAPTER SUMMARY

Mindful monetization isn't about extracting value from your community—it's about creating a fair exchange that fuels deeper transformation for your members and sustainable growth for you.

By focusing on transformation, you deliver value (not just features), in the process creating a strategic value ladder and tracking the metrics that matter. In this way, you'll build a community that thrives financially while staying true to its purpose.

Your community has the power to change lives. Price accordingly and watch the positive impact build.

CHAPTER 7 WORKSHEET

Blueprint for Mindful Monetization

PART 1: YOUR TRANSFORMATION STORY

Describe your community's transformation journey.

Before joining, members feel _____.

After ninety days, members will _____.

After one year, members will _____.

PART 2: VALUE LADDER DESIGN

Sketch your community's value tiers.

Free Tier

Primary value: _____

Key features:

1. _____
2. _____
3. _____

Success indicator: _____

Core Membership

Monthly price: $_____

Primary value: _____

Key features:

1. _____
2. _____
3. _____
4. _____
5. _____

Success indicator: _____

Premium Tier

Monthly price: $_____ (monthly or one-time)

Primary value: _____

Key features:

1. _____
2. _____
3. _____

Success indicator: _____

PART 3: METRICS TRACKER

Create your monthly metrics dashboard.

Engagement metrics:

Active members: _____

Engagement rate: _____%

Most popular content: _____

Financial metrics:

Total revenue: $_____

Revenue per member: $_____

Cost per acquisition: $_____

Transformation metrics:

Member success stories: _____

Transformation rate: _____%

Most common outcome: _____

PART 4: YOUR THIRTY-DAY ACTION PLAN
Your next steps.

Week 1: _____

Week 2: _____

Week 3: _____

Week 4: _____

One big goal for next month:

_____

_____

LOOKING AHEAD

Your community's financial health enables your mission's impact. When you deliver transformation, monetization becomes a natural extension of your value.

Now that we've established how to mindfully monetize your community and measure what truly matters, it's time to look toward the future. In Chapter 8, we'll explore how to create a kickass legacy for your community, building systems, and a culture that will thrive long after you've stepped back.

Get ready to learn how the most successful communities evolve from founder-dependent to community-powered ecosystems, creating impact that spans generations.

Ready to take your community engagement to the next level? Let's connect on LinkedIn and build something extraordinary together.

CHAPTER 8

NURTURING YOUR THRIVING ONLINE COMMUNITY

"The greatness of a community is most accurately measured by the compassionate actions of its members."

—Coretta Scott King

Congratulations, community builder. You've journeyed through seven chapters of strategies, insights, and real-world examples that illuminate how to build a kickass online community. You've clarified your purpose, designed a compelling culture, led with authenticity, structured engagement, explored scalable growth, balanced monetization, and learned how to measure the metrics that matter.

But here's the beautiful truth: Community building isn't a single race with a finish line. It's an ongoing adventure, sustained by your dedication to nurture, maintain, and keep evolving what you've created. This final chapter focuses on exactly that: How to care for and strengthen your online community so it remains vibrant, resilient, and ready for the future.

Let's explore how to maintain momentum and handle the inevitable changes that come with growth and time—all while keeping your community absolutely kickass.

1. KEEP THE FIRE OF PURPOSE BURNING: REMEMBER YOUR WHY

In *Chapter 1*, we discussed how we can use community to find a way forward for people in the digital environment that can potentially provide meaningful connections, a way out of our remote and hybrid lives to find our people and actively connect and build a meaningful community space. In *Chapter 2*, we explored how a clear purpose works like a North Star, providing navigation and supporting your community structural choices. The same principle applies in maintenance mode. People don't drift away because they're bored; they drift away when they're not reminded of the larger mission.

Continue to reiterate why your community exists through:

- Regular purpose-driven storytelling in your posts, emails, or newsletter intros.

- Refreshed onboarding materials that capture your evolving vision while staying true to core values.

- Milestone celebrations that connect achievements back to your shared purpose.

Purpose amplification tactic. Create a Purpose in Action monthly feature where you spotlight how specific members are living out the community's mission. This reinforces why you all came together while also celebrating real people making real impact.

As Brendon Burchard, founder of Growth Day, reminds us: "Community isn't just about belonging to something; it's about creating that sense of belonging for others. When you build a community with purpose, you're not just creating connections, you're crafting the future of human interaction."

2. CULTURE AS AN EVERYDAY PRACTICE

Culture isn't something you establish once and check off your list, it requires consistent nurturing to thrive. The vibrant community culture you designed in *Chapter 3* needs intentional care like this:

- Evolve your rituals to keep them fresh while maintaining their core meaning.

- Spotlight contributions that exemplify your values, showing members that culture matters.

- Periodically revisit guidelines with community input through "culture check-in" conversations.

Famed anthropologist Margaret Mead once said, "Never doubt that a small group of thoughtful, committed citizens can change the world; indeed, it's the only thing that ever has." Your community culture is the foundation for that change.

Culture reinforcement tactic. Schedule quarterly Values in Action challenges where members share how they're applying community values in their work and lives. This makes abstract values tangible and applicable.

When addressing issues that arise, remember Loretta J. Ross's principle: "Calling in is simply a call-out done with love." Approach members with curiosity and care rather than judgment whenever you need to address behaviors that don't align with your community values.

3. LEADERSHIP THAT INVITES PARTICIPATION

From **Chapter 4**, we discussed that leadership in an online community is about empowering others. As your community matures, your role should evolve from "the leader" to "a leader among many."

This is how to elevate members to leadership roles:

1. **Identify rising stars:** Notice who consistently shows up for others, shares valuable insights, or nurtures meaningful conversations.

2. **Create leadership pathways:** Design clear opportunities for members to take on increasing responsibility.

3. **Develop a leadership circle:** Form a core group of committed members who help guide the community's direction.

Leadership expansion tactic. Launch a Community Champions program, where experienced members can apply for (or be nominated to) specialized roles that match their strengths, for instance, content curators, welcome ambassadors, event hosts, or expertise guides.

Seth Godin says, "You don't find customers for your products; you find products for your customers." Translated to community life: You don't find leaders for your group; you discover leadership within the people already showing up, then help them expand that role.

4. ENGAGEMENT AS AN EVOLVING TAPESTRY

Chapter 5 highlighted structured activities to keep conversations lively and members engaged. Even the best engagement tactics can grow stale if not refreshed. Keep your community vibrant by:

- Rotating content series to maintain freshness (pause your Monday Motivation for a month and introduce Case Study Mondays).

- Encouraging member-led initiatives where passionate participants develop and lead new engagement formats.

- Establishing feedback loops through quick polls and thoughtful conversations about what's working.

Engagement evolution tactic. Create an Engagement Innovation Lab, where members can develop prototypes and test new interaction formats in small groups before rolling them out communitywide.

The future of community engagement lies at the intersection of digital and physical experiences. Consider developing:

- **Hybrid gatherings:** Virtual events with coordinated local meetups

- **Digital-physical challenges:** Online learning paired with real-world implementation

- **Geo-based subgroups:** Regional clusters within your global community

Remember that AI will increasingly handle the administrative aspects of community management, personalized recommendations, content curation, member matching. It can't, however, replace the authentic human connection at the heart of your community. Use technology to free up time for what truly matters: fostering meaningful relationships.

5. GROWING WITH SOUL: BALANCING NEWCOMERS AND FAMILIAR FACES

As your community scales (**Chapter 6**), maintaining warmth and connection becomes both more challenging and more important. Here's how to grow without losing your soul:

- **Implement welcome circles:** Pair new members with community veterans who can provide a friendly introduction.

- **Create meaningful subgroups:** Break larger communities into interest-based or experience-level circles.

- **Balance new energy with established wisdom:** Celebrate newcomers while honoring longtime members.

Soulful growth tactic. Develop a Community Journey Map that visualizes the ideal path from newcomer to established member to community leader, with clear milestones and experiences along the way.

Madhavi Jagdish, community leader extraordinaire, shares: "The most successful communities I've built don't focus on adding members; they focus on deepening connections. When you do that well, growth happens organically through word of mouth."

6. TENDING TO MONETIZATION AND METRICS WITH CARE

Money conversations (**Chapter 7**) are essential for sustainability and should always align with your community's purpose and values. As your monetization strategy matures:

1. *Maintain radical transparency:* Regularly share how community funds are being used to create value.

2. ***Evolve your offerings:*** Adjust pricing tiers and benefits based on member feedback and changing needs.

3. ***Balance accessibility with sustainability:*** Ensure that financial barriers don't exclude valuable voices while generating enough resources to thrive.

Mindful monetization tactic. Create an annual Community Investment Report showing how member contributions translated into community improvements, new offerings, and increased impact.

Even free communities need resource planning. Consider volunteer recognition programs, micro sponsorships, or collaborative grant applications if membership fees aren't part of your model.

7. MEASURING SUCCESS OVER THE LONG HAUL

You've learned to value meaningful metrics over vanity numbers (**Chapter 7**). As your community matures, evolve how you measure health:

- **Track transformation stories:** Collect and categorize specific examples of how your community changes lives.

- **Measure relationship density:** Map connections between members to visualize your community network.

- **Monitor leadership emergence:** Track how many members step into formal or informal leadership roles.

Holistic measurement tactic. Implement quarterly Community Pulse Checks that combine quantitative metrics with qualitative insights from member interviews, creating a richer picture of community health.

Set up periodic reviews, monthly, quarterly, or semiannually, where you examine both numbers and narratives to refine your strategy and celebrate progress.

8. FACING THE FUTURE WITH OPTIMISM AND ADAPTABILITY

The digital landscape evolves rapidly, platforms shift, algorithms change, new tools emerge. Your adaptability will determine your community's longevity:

- **Stay platform-agnostic:** Focus on building relationships that can thrive regardless of where they're hosted. Alternatively, go all in on your platform and request feature updates as needed.

- **Experiment with emerging tools:** Carefully test new technologies that might enhance your community experience.

- **Plan for succession and evolution:** Develop systems that will outlast any single leader, including yourself.

Future-readiness tactic. Form a small Horizon Team of forward-thinking members who regularly explore emerging community trends and technologies, bringing the best ideas back to the wider group.

Community expert Rosie Sherry notes: "The communities that thrive over the long term are the ones that stay true to their purpose while being willing to experiment with how they fulfill that purpose."

9. CREATING YOUR LEGACY PLAN

Every great community builder eventually thinks about legacy, how your community will continue to thrive even as your role evolves:

1. *Document your community's DNA:* Capture the essential elements that make your community special.

2. *Develop leadership redundancy:* Ensure multiple people understand each critical function.

3. *Create transition pathways:* Design clear processes for leadership evolution and knowledge transfer.

Legacy-building tactic. Create a Community Playbook that documents your most successful practices, cultural traditions, and operational systems so they can be preserved and adapted by future leaders.

The greatest legacy isn't a community that needs you forever, it's a community so well-designed that it continues to thrive even as leadership evolves.

GUIDING QUESTIONS

1. What specific elements of your community culture do you want to still be thriving five years from now? How are you actively preserving and strengthening those elements today?

2. What systems have you created that would allow your community to function effectively if you needed to step away for a month? What gaps need to be addressed?

3. How might your community's purpose evolve while staying true to its core values as your members grow and change over time?

4. What emerging technologies or cultural shifts might impact your community in the next few years? How can you prepare to adapt while preserving what makes your community special?

5. If you were to write a letter to your community one year from today celebrating your collective accomplishments, what specific achievements would you most want to highlight?

PODCAST RECOMMENDATIONS

NOTE: These podcasts and videos were accessible at the time of writing in March 2025. If you aren't finding the specific episode, try searching for similar content on YouTube.

• The Community-Led Growth Show, Episode 42 with Rosie Sherry on "Building Communities That Outlast Their Founders" explores practical succession planning and creating self-sustaining community systems.

• In Masters of Community, David Spinks interviews long-running community leaders in Episode 17, *"Decade-long Communities: Lessons from Leaders Who've Gone the Distance,"* revealing insights about building sustainable communities.

FAQS

1. How do I maintain my own energy and enthusiasm as a community leader over the long term?

Community leadership is a marathon, not a sprint. Establish clear boundaries around your time and energy, delegate responsibilities to trusted members, schedule regular inspiration days to reconnect with your purpose, and build a personal support network of fellow community leaders. Most important, remember that your community should energize you, not drain you. If it's consistently depleting, something needs to change in your approach. Connect with yourself deeply. Meditation or journaling could be a path for you. Most important, though: Become more intentional with all your actions.

2. **What's the best way to handle a community that seems to be losing momentum?**

First, gather data through both metrics and conversations to understand the root causes. Then, host an honest conversation with your most engaged members about what's shifting. Consider a community reset with a special event or challenge to reignite engagement. Sometimes, you need to prune what's not working, discontinue low-energy activities and double down on what sparks enthusiasm. Finally, revisit your purpose and make sure all activities directly connect to the transformation members seek.

3. **How do I handle the transition if I need to step away from leadership?**

Start planning your succession strategy long before you need it. Identify and develop multiple potential leaders, document your processes and community knowledge, and gradually shift responsibilities while you're still present to provide guidance. When it's time to transition, be transparent with your community about the changes, celebrate what you've built together, and create a clear handoff process. Consider maintaining a connection as an adviser or elder rather than disappearing completely.

4. **My community platform is changing its features and pricing. How do I navigate this disruption?**

Focus first on what makes your community special beyond any platform, your purpose, people, and culture. Communicate transparently with members about the changes and involve them in exploring options. Research alternatives thoroughly, prioritizing what matters most to your specific community. When transitioning platforms, move in phases with a core group testing the new environment first. Remember that some member loss is normal during transitions, and a well-managed change can ultimately strengthen your community.

5. How do I keep long-time members engaged when we're constantly welcoming newcomers?

Create special roles and recognition for your veterans, such as mentorship opportunities, or an advisory board that helps shape community direction. Develop traditions that honor tenure while being inclusive of newcomers. Balance beginner content with advanced topics that challenge experienced members. Most important, regularly check in with longtimers individually; they want to feel seen and valued for their ongoing commitment.

CHAPTER SUMMARY: AN ONGOING INVITATION

Building a kickass community is only the beginning. The real magic lies in nurturing the community so that it remains robust, engaging, and transformative year after year.

Keep focusing on quality connections, respect-filled communication, and constant evolution guided by your purpose. Remember that every small action you take, from welcoming a new member to celebrating a milestone, contributes to something extraordinary.

If you ever feel stuck, need a fresh perspective, or want to celebrate a victory, I'm here for you. Connect with me, Dr. Eve Kedar, on LinkedIn, to share your questions, challenges, or community wins. Part of my mission is supporting your mission. As your community thrives, we all rise together.

CHAPTER 8 WORKSHEET

Your Community Legacy and Vision for the Future

SECTION A: PURPOSE PRESERVATION AND EVOLUTION

Purpose clarity check

Your original purpose statement: _____

Is this still fully aligned with your community's direction?
☐ Yes   ☐ Needs refinement

If refinement is needed, update purpose:

_____

Purpose communication plan
How will you regularly reinforce your purpose? Select your strategies:

☐   Monthly purpose spotlight

☐   Purpose-aligned member stories

☐   Purpose check-in at events

☐   Visual purpose reminders

☐   Other: _____

SECTION B: CULTURE SUSTAINABILITY

Core values inventory
List the three to five most essential community values.

1. _____

2. _____

3. _____

4. _____

5. _____

Culture reinforcement system
For each value, identify one specific practice that reinforces it.

Value	Practice
1.	
2.	
3.	
4.	
5.	

Community traditions calendar
Map your key recurring traditions.

Weekly: _____

Monthly: _____

Quarterly: _____

Annually: _____

SECTION C: LEADERSHIP DEVELOPMENT

Leadership identification

Current active leaders: _____

Potential emerging leaders: _____

Leadership gaps to fill: _____

Leadership pathway design

Provide a few examples of entry-level leadership roles:

_____

_____

_____

Provide a few examples of intermediate leadership roles:

_____

_____

_____

Provide a few examples of advanced leadership roles:

_____

_____

_____

Your leadership evolution plan

Your current primary roles: _____

_____

Roles you'll transition away from: _____

_____

Roles you'll maintain over the long term: _____

_____

Timeline for transitions: _____

_____

SECTION D: ENGAGEMENT EVOLUTION

Engagement pattern analysis

List your three most successful engagement formats. For each format, how could you refresh or evolve it?

1. _____

2. _____

3. _____

New engagement experiments

List three new engagement formats to test. For each experiment, define your success metrics.

1. _____

2. _____

3. _____

SECTION E: FUTURE SUSTAINABILITY PLANNING

Resource assessment

Current sustainability model: _____

Resource gaps or concerns: _____

Potential new resource streams: _____

Technology transition planning

Current critical platforms: _____

Potential alternatives to explore: _____

Platform-independent assets: _____

Succession planning framework

List three critical functions requiring documentation:

1. _____

2. _____

3. _____

List your current knowledge transfer methods:

_____

_____

_____

_____

_____

_____

SECTION F: YOUR NINETY-DAY LEGACY BUILDING PLAN

Month 1: Documentation and systems
Plan and calendar your key actions.

_____

_____

_____

_____

_____

Month 2: Leadership development
What actions are you taking in the next 30–60–90 days to level up your leadership.

_____

_____

_____

_____

Month 3: Future innovation
Are you integrating generative AI tools? What ideas are sparked for you to leverage in your community

One-year vision statement:

One year from today, our community will _____

_____

CHAPTER 9

EPILOGUE

"The power of human connection is that it can stretch across time and distance, each relationship becoming a thread in the fabric of our collective future."

—Brené Brown

By choosing to build and maintain an online community, you've answered that question beautifully. You're creating a haven where others can grow, learn, transform, and connect. Whether it's ten members or ten thousand, your dedication to making people feel valued, supported, and inspired is a profound gift to the world.

Building a legacy isn't about making your community depend on you forever—it's about creating something so meaningful and well-structured that it continues to thrive and evolve with or without your daily presence. The greatest community builders create spaces that outlast them.

Keep going! Keep your eyes on the horizon and your heart with your people. Even if you can't do all the great things at once, every small act of nurturing and every intentional conversation adds up to something truly meaningful.

Indeed, your community has the power to change lives, spark movements, and create ripples of transformation that extend far beyond your membership roster. That's not just kickass, that's your gift to the world. Make it meaningful and make it last.

I look forward to connecting with you and continuing the conversation. And I can't wait to see how you and your community soar!

With gratitude and excitement for your journey,

Dr. Eve Kedar

Ready to take your community engagement to the next level? Let's connect on LinkedIn and build something extraordinary together.

RESOURCES AND TOOLS

COMMUNITY-ORIENTED PODCASTS

NOTE: These podcasts and videos were accessible at the time of writing, in March 2025.

1. *Building Community with Ilana Golan (30–45 min)*

Host: Ilana Golan

Why listen: A dynamic podcast that balances theory with real-world application. Ilana brings her experience as a tech leader and community builder, sharing actionable insights through engaging, storyteller-style episodes. Great for both beginners and pros seeking inspiration and practical tips.

Link: https://podcasts.apple.com/us/podcast/leap-academy-with-ilana-golan/id1701718200

2. *The Tim Ferriss Show (1.5–2 hours)*

Host: Tim Ferriss

Why listen: Though not exclusively about community building, Tim's deep-dive interviews often feature thought leaders who excel at building tribes and movements, such as Seth Godin. The longer format allows for a nuanced exploration of strategies behind thriving communities in various domains.

Link: tim.blog/podcast

3. Masters of Community (45–60 min)

Host: David Spinks

Why listen: David Spinks (of CMX) brings years of community-building expertise to the table. Each episode offers a potent mix of strategic thinking and tactical advice, with diverse guests from different industries and community types—perfect for discovering new engagement approaches.

Link: Content can be found on YouTube.

4. Community Signal (45 min)

Host: Patrick O'Keefe

Why listen: No-fluff conversations focusing on real challenges in moderating and growing online communities. Patrick cuts straight to implementation details, making this ideal for those who want to solve everyday community-management issues with clear, expert-backed strategies.

Link: communitysignal.com

5. The Community Lab (30–40 min)

Host: Various industry experts

Why listen: Short, focused episodes each tackling a specific community-building challenge or strategy. Perfect for busy managers seeking quick, actionable insights. Listen, then immediately apply the lessons to your own community.

Link: communityroundtable.com/category/podcast/

NOTE: Episodes and naming may vary; some are featured under The Community Roundtable's umbrella.

6. Akimbo (20–30 min)

Host: Seth Godin

Why listen: Seth Godin's unique storytelling style and marketing expertise make community concepts accessible and memorable. Expect shorter episodes packed with paradigm-shifting ideas that challenge how you approach community engagement and leadership.

Link: akimbo.link

7. The Community Corner (40–50 min)

Host: The Commsor team

Why listen: Commsor's show stands out for its focus on metrics, ROI, and the strategic elements of community building. Perfect for professionals who need to justify and measure community investments in a business context.

Link: commsor.com/resources/podcasts/
the-community-corner

8. Building Brand Communities (45–50 min)

Hosts: Carrie Melissa Jones and Charles Vogl

Why listen: A deep exploration into how strong communities are crucial for brand success. Features case studies from both household names and smaller businesses, offering universal lessons on loyalty, trust, and meaningful engagement.

Link: https://theconversationfactory.com/podcast/
communities-are-conversations

9. Get Together (30–45 min)

Hosts: Bailey Richardson, Kevin Huynh, and Kai Elmer Sotto (People & Company)

Why listen: Focuses on how people unite for shared passions or values. Through real-life examples—from small meetup groups to large-scale fandoms—this show uncovers the psychology and practical methods that spark and sustain vibrant communities.

Link: peopleand.company/podcast

10. Conversations with Bacon (45–60 min)

Host: Jono Bacon

Why listen: Jono Bacon is a seasoned tech and open-source community manager (Ubuntu, GitHub, XPRIZE). Each episode features candid interviews with community managers, tech leaders, and innovators, providing firsthand insights on scaling, contributor engagement, and cultivating inclusive spaces.

Link: jonobacon.com/conversations

11. The Community Experience (40–50 min)

Hosts: The SPI Media Team (Jill and Tony)

Why listen: Produced by the minds behind Smart Passive Income, this podcast dives into how community fuels online business growth. Topics range from platform selection and membership models to forging meaningful connections that impact your bottom line.

Link: smartpassiveincome.com/podcasts/ the-community-experience

12. The Community Collective Podcast (30–40 min)

Host: Rotating panel of community experts

Why listen: A panel-style format tackling issues like conflict resolution, scaling, or reengaging dormant members from multiple angles. Great for hearing varied perspectives, which makes each discussion adaptable to different types or sizes of communities.

Link: communitycollective.show. Or search your podcast app if the domain changes.

13. Community Alchemy (20–30 min)

Host: Various guest hosts and community builders

Why listen: Short, insightful episodes on the alchemy of converting passive groups into tight-knit communities. Focuses on interpersonal dynamics—motivation, empathy, and group psychology—that spark genuine engagement and loyalty.

Link:

- Pod.link/CommunityAlchemy (This may be redirected to various listening platforms.)

- Alternatively, check major podcast apps for Community Alchemy.

HOW THEY ALL FIT TOGETHER

- Long-form, in-depth interviews (e.g., The Tim Ferriss Show and Masters of Community) help you dive into nuanced strategies.

- Short, tactical episodes (Online Community Results, Community Alchemy) provide on-the-go insights for quick implementation.

- Brand and business-focused (Building Brand Communities, The Community Corner) guide you on ROI and corporate value.

- Niche and tech-savvy (Conversations with Bacon, InSecurity) show you how to engage specialized audiences effectively.

With these 13 podcasts, featuring everything from theoretical frameworks to real-world case studies, you'll gain a well-rounded education in building and sustaining your own kickass online community. Note: These links worked when writing this book (March, 2025). Check for similar content on YouTube if the podcast is no longer active. Happy listening!

GUIDELINES, TEMPLATES, AND EXAMPLES

FOR CHAPTER 2

Template for Community Purpose Statement

[Community Name] Purpose Statement

Our community, [name], exists to [core purpose]. We aim to [key outcome or transformation you enable] for [target audience or ideal member persona].

Through [key activities, resources, experiences you provide], we help our members [specific benefits or value]. Together, we're [larger vision, mission, or movement].

Our community commitments:

- [Value or principle 1]

- [Value or principle 2]

- [Value or principle 3]

What makes us unique:

[Brief description of your community's unique approach, focus, or style]

Guiding questions

- How does this align with and support our community's purpose?

- Will this help our members achieve [core transformation or outcome]?

- Does this strengthen the relationships and culture within our community?

> **Use this purpose statement** to guide your community's strategy, decisions, and actions. Regularly communicate and reinforce it with members. As your community evolves, revisit and refine your purpose to ensure continued relevance and resonance.

Template for Welcome Statement

Welcome to [community name]!

Hello, [new member name].

We're thrilled to have you join us in [community name]! You're now part of a vibrant group of [shared interest/profession/goal].

What you can expect:

- [Key benefit/offering 1]

- [Key benefit/offering 2]

- [Key benefit/offering 3]

Getting started:

1. [First step/action]

2. [Second step/action]

3. [Third step/action]

Community Resources

- [Resource 1]

- [Resource 2]

- [Resource 3]

Get involved

We encourage you to jump in and [key action, e.g., introduce yourself, ask a question, share a resource]. The more you participate, the more value you'll gain from being part of this community.

If you have any questions, feel free to reach out to [contact name/ info]. We're here to help you make the most of your [community name] experience!

Welcome aboard,

[Your name]

[Your role, e.g., Community Leader/Manager/Founder]

P.S. As a special welcome gift, [includes a welcome offering, e.g., downloadable resource, discount code, invitation to special event].

> **Note this template should be used as a guideline.** You need to customize the message and welcome activities as appropriate to your community. These can range from a live meeting, video messages, a scavenger hunt to orient the new members to the community, and additional verbiage as needed.

[community name] Moderator

[community name] Moderation Guidelines:

Welcome to [community name]! To ensure a positive, productive, and supportive environment for all members, we have established the following moderation guidelines.

Guiding principles

- Be respectful and inclusive

- Foster meaningful discussions

- Protect privacy and safety

- Encourage authentic engagement

- Uphold our community values of [list core values]

Community standards

- No hate speech, discrimination, or personal attacks

- No spam, self-promotion, or irrelevant content

- Respect intellectual property rights; no plagiarism

- Use trigger warnings and content labels as needed

- Add other specific rules relevant to your community]

Moderation process

1. Moderators actively monitor discussions for potential issues

2. Members can flag concerning content for review

3. Moderators assess flagged content based on guidelines

4. Actions taken may include:

   - Removal of content
   - Warning to member
   - Temporary or permanent suspension of membership

5. Decisions are communicated clearly to affected members

6. Appeals process: [Explain how members can appeal moderation decisions]

Moderator commitments

- Treat all members fairly and consistently

- Maintain confidentiality in moderation matters

- Engage in ongoing training and discussion to ensure alignment

- Be open to feedback and continuously improve our processes

We believe in taking a firm but compassionate approach, assuming positive intent while acting to protect the integrity of our community.

By participating in [community name], all members agree to abide by these moderation guidelines. We appreciate your cooperation in cocreating a community we can all be proud of.

FOR CHAPTER 3

Our Community Guidelines

> **NOTE:** These guidelines are illustrative examples; we encourage you to customize and adapt them to align with your community's unique purpose, values, and goals.

Welcome to [your community name]! We're excited to have you as part of our vibrant and supportive community. To ensure a positive experience for all members, we ask that you adhere to the following guidelines:

1. Be respectful and inclusive.

- Treat all members with kindness, respect, and empathy.
- Embrace diversity in all its forms, and actively work to create a welcoming, inclusive environment for all.
- Be open to different perspectives and engage in constructive discussions.

2. Foster meaningful conversations.

- Share content that is relevant, valuable, and on-topic.
- Offer support, advice, and resources when appropriate.
- Stay curious and ask questions to deepen understanding.

3. Maintain a safe environment.

- Respect others' privacy and confidentiality.
- Refrain from sharing explicit, violent, or illegal content.
- Use content warnings for sensitive topics.

- Do not share conversations and/or content beyond this community without explicit permissions.

4. Promote collaboration, not competition.

- Celebrate others' successes and offer encouragement.
- Provide constructive feedback and avoid personal attacks.
- Give credit and recognition.
- No pitching, unless that is the topic of the day!

5. Respect intellectual property.

- Only share content that you have the right to share.
- Give proper attribution when referencing others' work.
- Do not plagiarize or infringe on copyrights.

6. Keep it spam-free.

- Focus on generous contributions that add value to the community. Avoid excessive self-promotion.
- Do not share unsolicited or irrelevant content.
- Respect others' boundaries and communication preferences.

7. Uphold community values

- Familiarize yourself with our community's mission and values.
- Act in a way that aligns with and supports these values.
- Hold yourself and others accountable to these standards.

Moderation and reporting

- We believe in "calling in" before "calling out." If you see behavior that doesn't align with our guidelines, consider reaching out to that member directly with compassion and empathy to explore the issue.

- If a direct conversation isn't feasible or the behavior continues, please report it to our moderation team via [reporting instructions].

- Our moderation team is here to ensure a safe and positive community experience.

- If you encounter any content or behavior that violates these guidelines, please report it to [reporting instructions].

- Moderators will review reports promptly and take appropriate action, which may include removing content, issuing warnings, or revoking membership.

- By participating in [your community name], you agree to abide by these guidelines. We reserve the right to update these guidelines as needed to maintain a healthy community environment.

- If you have any questions or concerns, please reach out to [contact information]. Thank you for being a valued member of our community!

GUIDE TO COMMUNITY MANAGEMENT SOFTWARE OPTIONS

Options often change when new platforms emerge, and current (as of spring 2025) platforms merge or close. Please use this as a guide, and be sure to do your research and due diligence. Make sure the platform syncs with your strategy. The platforms are presented in alphabetical order, not in order of preference or importance.

1. CIRCLE.SO

- **Established:** 2019
- **Key features:** White-label, customization, monetization, integrations
- **Ideal for:** Creator communities, membership sites, course communities
- **Pricing:** Starts at $39/month
- **Con:** Lacks some advanced features like built-in live streaming

2. DISCORD

- **Established:** 2015
- **Key features:** Voice/video chat, screen sharing, live streaming, bots
- **Ideal for:** Gaming communities, fan groups, casual communities

- **Pricing:** Free for basic features; paid plans start at $9.99/month
- **Con:** Limited moderation tools compared to other platforms

3. DISCOURSE

- **Established:** 2013
- **Key features:** Open-source, customization, moderation tools, single sign-on
- **Ideal for:** Developer communities, open-source projects, large-scale forums
- **Pricing:** Free self-hosted; managed plans start at $100/month
- **Con:** Requires technical expertise for self-hosting and customization

4. HIGHER LOGIC

- **Established:** 2007
- **Key features:** Automation, gamification, volunteer management, analytics
- **Ideal for:** Associations, user groups, customer communities
- **Pricing:** Available upon request
- **Con:** More expensive than other options, geared towards larger organizations

5. HIVEBRITE

- **Established:** 2015

- **Key features:** CRM integration, events, membership management, mobile apps

- **Ideal for:** Alumni groups, nonprofits, professional networks

- **Pricing:** Starts at $500/month

- **Con:** Higher starting price point than other platforms

6. MAVEN

- **Established:** 2020

- **Key features:** White-label, cohorts, live sessions, course creation

- **Ideal for:** Cohort-based courses, coaching communities, professional development

- **Pricing:** Starts at $25/month

- **Con:** Newer platform may have fewer integrations and customization options.

7. MIGHTY NETWORKS

- **Established:** 2017

- **Key features:** Website builder, mobile apps, course creation, live streaming

- **Ideal for:** Creators, coaches, entrepreneurs, brands

- **Pricing:** Starts at $33/month
- **Con:** Limited customization compared to white-label platforms

8. NAS.IO

- **Established:** 2019
- **Key features:** Customizable profiles, content creation tools, event management, analytics
- **Ideal for:** Niche communities, knowledge sharing, professional networks
- **Pricing:** Starts at $99/month
- **Con:** Less-established brand recognition compared to other platforms

9. SKOOL

- **Established:** 2021
- **Key features:** White-label, mobile apps, live streaming, gamification
- **Ideal for:** Educational communities, cohort-based courses, membership sites
- **Pricing:** Starts at $149/month
- **Con:** Relatively new platform, may have fewer integration options

10. SLACK

- **Established:** 2013

- **Key features:** Real-time messaging, voice/video calls, integrations, file sharing

- **Ideal for:** Professional communities, remote teams, customer support

- **Pricing:** Free for basic features; paid plans start at $6.67/user/month

- **Con:** Not designed specifically for community building, can get noisy

11. TRIBE

- **Established:** 2015

- **Key Features:** White-label, customization, mobile apps, monetization

- **Ideal For:** Creator communities, brands, entrepreneurs

- **Pricing:** Starts at $59/month

- **Con:** Some technical bugs and performance issues reported by users

12. VANILLA FORUMS

- **Established:** 2009

- **Key features:** Customization, gamification, ideation, Q&A, analytics

- **Ideal for:** Customer communities, large-scale forums

- **Pricing:** Starts at $689/month

- **Con:** Higher price point than many other platforms

When selecting a community management platform, carefully consider your budget, required features, and the level of technical expertise you have available. Take advantage of free trials when possible and verify that the platform you choose provides responsive customer support and regular updates to meet your community's evolving needs.

GLOSSARY

A

Active participants: Members who regularly engage in community activities, contribute generously, participate in discussions. Support the community's culture. You want more of these!

Accountability partnerships: Structured relationship between community members who help each other stay on track with goals.

Action takers: Readers or community members who are ready to dive in, contribute, and make real changes. They show up consistently, share insights, and help spark momentum in a group.

Affiliation: The sense of belonging and connection members feel toward the community and each other.

Authentic networking: An approach to building relationships based on genuine interest, empathy, and mutual support, rather than transactional or spammy tactics.

B

Bacon, Jono: A seasoned community strategist and author who often discusses how to empower community leaders and distribute responsibility so the group can scale without losing its heart. Find on YouTube

Belonging: A fundamental human need to feel connected, accepted, and valued. In an online community context, belonging emerges when members feel seen and heard, fostering deeper engagement and loyalty.

Bianchini, Gina: Founder of Mighty Networks. She famously notes, "A community is the single most powerful way to navigate a highly dynamic, rapidly changing world." Bianchini advocates creating not just online "content," but true online "connection." She can be found on YouTube.

Burchard, Brendon: A high-performance coach and creator of the Growth Day community. Known for his energetic teaching style and focus on personal development, Brendon's work often illustrates how a well-structured, purpose-driven space can unite people around self-improvement. He has used multiple platforms. Currently he can be found on a customized version of Circle.so.

Buddy system: A community program that pairs new members with experienced ones for orientation and support. Some systems, such as Mighty Networks, are leveraging AI tools to share similarly profiled members with each other to encourage connections.

C

The Carbon Almanac: The book, The Carbon Almanac: It's not too late, is a powerful tool to help people understand the complexity of the global climate crisis and recommends actions for all of us. Includes a foreword by Seth Godin. Offers free resources for teachers, parents, and groups. https://thecarbonalmanac.org/book/

ChatBlackGPT and Erin Reddick: Erin Reddick is dedicated to empowering and educating all of us about generative AI and inclusivity. ChatBlackGPT is revolutionizing AI diversity. For more, see https://chatblackgpt.com and YouTube.

Circle.so: A popular community platform offering customizable spaces, courses, live events, and discussion threads. Used by entrepreneurs and creators who want a more "white-labeled" environment than social media groups.

Community: A group of people united by a shared purpose, interest, or goal, actively supporting each other's growth and sense of belonging. A community thrives on genuine interaction and shared experiences.

Community culture: The shared values, behaviors, practices, and even beliefs that define how members interact and engage. You want to model your desired community culture, remind your members of expectations, and reinforce these as appropriate to your community to build a cohesive culture.

Community guidelines: The behavioral codes and values that outline how members should interact. Clear guidelines help maintain a safe, respectful environment and protect the community's culture. Clear consequences keep your community members safe and builds trust. An example is available in the template section.

Connection catalysts: Activities or features designed to spark meaningful relationships between members.

Community manager: A person (or team) responsible for fostering engagement, moderating discussions, and ensuring the community's culture and values remain strong.

Culture: The "personality" of the community, shaped by shared values, norms, traditions, and rituals that guide how members interact and feel about the space.

D

Discord: A chat-based platform originally designed for gamers but now used widely across industries. Allows real-time voice, video, and text communication, making it a flexible tool for community-building.

Discourse: An open-source software platform designed for building online communities. Founded by Jeff Atwood, Robin Ward, and Sam Saffron and officially released in August 2014. Seth Godin's Purple Space is hosted on this platform. Provides a trust level system, tagging, and rich categorization features.

E

Energy bringers : Members who consistently contribute positively to the community atmosphere and inspire others.

Engagement architecture: A structured plan or rhythm (daily, weekly, monthly) that fosters meaningful participation. It can include prompts, challenges, events, or rituals that encourage members to interact consistently and deeply. It is the structured framework for creating meaningful member participation and interaction.

Engagement engine: Systems and processes that drive consistent member participation and interactions.

F

FAQs: Frequently Asked Questions with answers you can find at the end of each chapter.

Free-tier foundations: Basic community features and benefits available to all members without cost.

Forde, Eva MSSW: A brilliant founding member in Seth Godin's Purple Space, who underscores the importance of repeating community values. A project leader for The Carbon Almanac, she has founded the Social Work Wealth Conference helping social workers monetize their knowledge and skills. https://www.evaforde.com/

Fun!: What you and your members should all be having as part of belonging to your community process. Even if it is a serious community with professional goals, fun should always find a way in.

G

Gamification: The use of game-like elements (e.g., points, badges, leaderboards) to motivate participation. When done thoughtfully, it can boost engagement; when forced, it can feel gimmicky.

Godin, Seth: Brilliant and generous marketing guru, author of This is Strategy, and founding editor of The Carbon Almanac. He champions the ideas of tribes, minimal viable audiences, and making meaningful contributions. He urges community builders to "find your people" because "people like us do things like this." Find amazing interviews and content on YouTube and at https://seths.blog/.

Golan, Ilana: Leader of Leap Academy and host of the Leap Academy podcast. The academy provides leadership training, including public speaking and supports people taking their next leap. https://www.leapacademy.com/

H

Happe, Rachel: Cofounder of The Community Roundtable. Often highlights how communities are not about technology alone, but about the shared purpose and value they create. Find her on YouTube at Cultivating Communities with Rachel Happe of Community Roundtable.

High-touch offerings: Premium community experiences involving direct access to leadership or specialized support.

Humor: Never underestimate the power of appropriate humor in many community situations. It can defuse conflict and instill a sense of joy.

Hope: A well-designed community brings hope to the members. This is the shared belief in a better future. Hope can be fostered through collective effort, mutual support, and a sense of belonging. Hope is the driving force that encourages individuals to engage, collaborate, and invest in the well-being of the community. Hope creates resilience, inspires action, and inspires action, even in the face of challenges.

I

Impact dashboard: A collection of metrics that measure meaningful community outcomes and transformation.

Implementation framework: Structured approach for putting community strategies into action.

J

Jones, Carrie Melissa: A leading community consultant who emphasizes the importance of creating experiences over just pushing content. She often reminds community leaders to be hosts rather than stars of the show.

Jasper: Community.jasper.ai: A well-developed Circle.so community. Take a look at how the content is organized and how easy it is to find content.

K

Karch, Louise: An advocate and Purple Space participant who underscores both generosity and the need for clarity in guidelines. The amazing author of Word Glue, Louise advises readers to, "Set community guidelines at the start." She also encourages empathy and curiosity when conflicts arise. She is also part of The Carbon Almanac project. https://www.wordglue.co/

Kedar, Dr. Eve: Author of this book, and happy to stay connected. Please reach out to me on LinkedIn or at my website evekedar.com to keep on building your kickass community.

King, Keith: An engaged and generous member of Seth Godin's Purple Space, Keith exemplifies how genuine relationships keep members returning, he stays in Purple Space for its rich sense of connection, not fancy features or marketing. His podcast, In Residence with Keith and Laura is available on Apple podcasts and wherever you find podcasts. https://withkeithandlaura.com

Kindred spirits: Those who share your passions, values, or goals. They often join a community seeking a deeper connection with "people like us" who understand their worldview.

King Jr., Dr. Martin Luther: Civil rights leader known for emphasizing our interconnectedness: "We are tied together in a single garment of destiny." His quote illustrates how belonging and mutual support are at the core of any thriving community, online or offline. TheKingCenter.org and on YouTube.

L

Leadership layers: Different levels of community leadership roles and responsibilities.

Leadership team: A group of members or volunteers who support the main community leader by moderating discussions, organizing events, and welcoming newcomers. Distributing leadership helps a community scale effectively.

Leap Academy: A professional and personal growth program lead by Ilana Golan. Her podcast and more content can be found on YouTube.

Legacy building: Activities focused on creating lasting community impact and value, beyond the current leadership.

M

Matei, Catalin: A podcast host and interviewer who has featured Gina Bianchini and other community-building experts who explore how to spark meaningful connection online. Find him on YouTube.

Member journey: The progression of experiences from joining to becoming an established community member.

Member onboarding: The process of welcoming and orienting new members. Effective onboarding introduces them to the community's purpose, culture, and guidelines, helping them contribute and feel at home quickly.

Microcommunities: Smaller, focused groups that can exist within the larger community. Similar to "birds of a feather" or affiliation groups. Can be used for special projects. Smaller subgroups or cohorts within a larger community, formed around specific interests or goals. They foster closer bonds and a more intimate feel, even as the main group scales.

Mighty Networks: All-in-one community platform allowing creators to host courses, events, and group discussions under their own branding. Gina Bianchini's creation.

Millington, Richard: Founder of FeverBee, known for stating, "A community isn't a place or platform; it's a feeling." He underscores how communities succeed when people feel that sense of belonging. Make your community indispensable on YouTube.

Mindful monetization: Thoughtful approach to generating revenue while maintaining community value and trust. Worth checking out bearcoaches.thrivecart.com for their anti-capitalist guide on this topic of pricing.

N

Nas.io: A platform that focuses on connecting niche communities around a shared purpose. Used by various creators who want a more guided approach to community-building.

O

O'Keefe, Patrick: Founder of iFroggy Network and a leading voice on digital community management. He reminds leaders that "the technology is interesting, but the human potential is revolutionary." https://www.managingcommunities.com/about/

Onboarding: The process of welcoming and orienting new members to your community. Helping them understand the culture, norms, and expectations. Making the environment friendly, inviting, and easy to navigate.

O'Neill, Rosemary: Cofounder of Social Strata. Emphasizes that successful online communities "build a home where people want to stay," focusing on emotional connection over purely technical solutions. Also findable on YouTube.

P

Paech, Venessa: One of Australia's leading experts in online communities. She emphasizes communities are built on stories, rituals, and shared experiences creating meaning.

Pantazis, Dr. Mary Ellen: Founder of TIC: Thrive, Include, Connect. A community built to foster a supportive online community for parents and educators of diverse learners. This is a safe space to ask questions, and find resources listed by US States. Reach out to Dr. Mary Ellen Pantazis on LinkedIn for an invite. https://tic_thriveincludeconnect.circle.so/c/start-here/welcome

Pisarski, Paz: Co-founder of The Community Collective, a global community for community builders. She specialized in building cohort-based communities using both "hard curriculum" and "hidden curriculum" approaches focused on creating belonging.

Posner, Amy: Business coach and mentor. Believer in the value of diversity in community membership. Find her on YouTube.

Premium experiences: Enhanced community offerings usually only available to members on higher-priced tiers.

Purple Space: A Discourse-based community by Seth Godin that emphasizes meaningful connection over flashy features. Known for its generous vibe and strong culture of mutual support. https://www.sethgodin.com/ and https://together.purple.space

Purpose: The why behind a community's existence, what transformation or shared goal unites its members. A clear purpose acts as the community's North Star, guiding decisions and engagement.

Purpose statement: Clear articulation of the community's reason for existing and intended impact.

Q

Quality controls: Systems for maintaining community standards during growth.

R

Reddick, Erin: Erin Reddick is dedicated to empowering and educating all of us about generative AI and inclusivity. ChatBlackGPT is revolutionizing AI diversity. For more information about ChatBlackGPT, check out https://chatblackgpt.com and YouTube.

Recognition systems: Structured ways to acknowledge and celebrate members, their contributions, achievements, birthdays, and more.

Reflection/guiding questions: Targeted prompts at the end of each chapter (or discussion) that help members (or readers) process information and apply insights to their own lives or projects.

Retention metrics: Measurement of how well the community keeps members engaged over time.

Rheingold, Howard: A pioneer in the field of virtual communities, emphasizing the revolutionary potential of humans connecting deeply across digital networks. Find him on YouTube.

Robbins, Tony: Motivational speaker who's said, "Setting goals is the first step in turning the invisible into the visible." This mindset aligns with building a "big purpose" for online communities, getting crystal clear on desired outcomes for members. Find him on YouTube.

Ross, Loretta J.: Author of *Calling In: How to Start Making Change With Those You'd Rather Cancel.* Known for her "calling in" techniques—advising leaders to approach challenging conversations with curiosity instead of shame, thereby preserving respect while handling disruptive behavior. Listen to her TED talk on YouTube.

Russell, Noelle: Founder of the I Heart AI community on Skool, centered on exploring AI's ethical implications. Demonstrates how a focused, mission-driven space can attract passionate members, even without massive numbers. https://noellerussell. ai

S

Safe space: An environment where members feel comfortable expressing themselves without fear of ridicule or harm. Achieved through clear guidelines, respectful leadership, and a supportive culture.

Sam (fictional name for a real community member): A Purple Space member who recommends "leaning in and seeking to understand" when conflicts arise, implying that curiosity often solves more problems than quick judgment.

Scaling with soul: Growing a community in a way that preserves its core values, culture, and sense of belonging, rather than chasing big numbers at the expense of genuine engagement.

Skool: A platform that integrates course hosting with community features. Popular among edupreneurs looking to merge learning and interaction seamlessly.

Small group architecture: Structure for organizing members into manageable, connected groups. Important for larger communities.

Spinks, David: Founder of CMX, a hub for community professionals. He stresses that community-building is about creating a space where people can do more together than they ever could alone. Find him on YouTube.

Stats on Stats podcast: Your source for all things cyber security and IT. Hosted by Jordyn Short and Tiffiny B. They host expert guests and are full of great energy. Check them out on wherever you play your podcasts and on YouTube.

Success indicators: Measurable signs that the community is achieving its goals. These can be specific to each type of community.

Support: One of the core pillars of thriving communities, where members celebrate wins, navigate challenges, and remind each other they're not alone.

T

TIC (Thrive Include Connect): A community built to foster a supportive online community for parents and educators of diverse learners. This is a safe space to ask questions, and find resources listed by US States. Reach out to Dr. Mary Ellen Pantazis on LinkedIn for an invite. https://tic_thriveincludeconnect.circle.so/c/start-here/welcome

Transformation: The process of meaningful change that members experience through their involvement in a community, whether that's personal growth, professional skills, or simply feeling more connected.

Transformation seekers: Individuals at pivotal life or career moments who crave guidance, accountability, and support. A strong community can offer them exactly what they need to grow.

Thought leaders: Experts or innovators who bring specialized knowledge and elevate community discussions. They often serve as mentors, content contributors, or moderators.

Trust-building elements: Features and practices that help develop confidence and security among members.

U

User-generated content (UGC): Content created and shared by community members, such as posts, comments, images, or videos.

V

Value architecture: The structured approach to delivering benefits across different membership tiers.

Value exchange mindset: Understanding community participation as a two-way flow of benefits.

Vogl, Charles: Author of The Art of Community. He highlights how ancient principles of belonging and ritual apply to modern online communities. You'll find him on YouTube.

W

Welcome Wagon: A group of more experienced community members who volunteer to greet and guide new members during their initial interactions.

Wiki: A collaborative website or document that allows community members to contribute, edit, and organize content around a specific topic or purpose.

X

XaaS (Everything as a Service): A term encompassing various service models, such as Software as a Service (SaaS), Platform as a Service (PaaS), and Infrastructure as a Service (IaaS), which can be used to host and manage community platforms.

X-Factor: A unique or exceptional quality that sets a community apart from others, making it attractive and valuable to its members.

Y

Yarn: A colloquial term for a long, detailed story or discussion thread within a community, often used to describe engaging or memorable conversations.

Z

Zeitgeist: The defining spirit or mood of a particular period, which can influence the topics, interests, and behaviors with a community.

Zoom fatigue: A term describing the exhaustion and burnout associated with participating in too many video conferences, which can impact virtual community engagement. As a community leader, kindly be mindful of this.

REFERENCES

The insights and strategies presented in this book draw primarily from in-depth interviews with community builders, engagement specialists, and organizational leaders who have successfully fostered thriving online communities. These firsthand accounts of challenges, innovations, and best practices form the backbone of the practical approach that defines this work. To ensure comprehensiveness and to validate these experiential findings, I supplemented interview data with extensive research from academic journals, industry publications, case studies, and contemporary texts on community building, user engagement, and digital collaboration. The following resources represent key references that informed my understanding and approach to building kickass online communities. They serve as excellent starting points for readers seeking to deepen their knowledge in specific areas of community development and engagement.

BOOKS

Bacon, Jono — *People Powered: How Communities Can Supercharge Your Business, Brand, and Teams*. New York: HarperCollins Leadership, 2019.

Block, Peter — *Community: The Structure of Belonging*. Oakland, CA: Berrett-Koehler, 2018.

Fowler, Jenny Li — *Organic Social Media: How to Build Flourishing Online Communities*. New York: Kogan Page, 2023.

Godin, Seth — *This Is Strategy: Make Better Plans (Create a Strategy to Elevate Your Career, Community & Life)*. New York: Authors Equity, 2024.

Jones Carrie, Melissa, and Vogl, Charles — *Building Brand Communities: How Organizations Succeed by Creating Belonging*. Oakland CA: Brett-Koehler Publishers, 2020.

Kedar, Eve — *Build a Kickass Sales Team: Practical Sales Tactics*. FL: GWN, 2025.

Kraut, Robert E., and Paul Resnick, eds — *Building Successful Online Communities: Evidence-Based Social Design*. Cambridge, MA: MIT Press, 2012.

Putnam, Robert D — *Bowling Alone: The Collapse and Revival of American Community*. New York: Simon & Schuster, 2000.

Rasmussen, Robert — *Better Places: Building Stronger Communities with Authenticity and Compassion*. Charleston, SC: Advantage Media Group, 2024.

Rheingold, Howard — *The Virtual Community: Homesteading on the Electronic Frontier*. Revised ed. Cambridge, MA: MIT Press, 2000.

Richardson, Bailey, Kevin Huynh, and Kai Elmer Sotto — *Get Together: How to Build a Community with Your People*. San Francisco: Stripe Press, 2019.

Ross, Loretta J — *Calling In: How to Start Making Change with Those You'd Rather Cancel*. New York: Simon & Schuster Digital Sales LLC, February 4, 2025.

Shirky, Clay — *Here Comes Everybody: The Power of Organizing Without Organizations*. New York: Penguin Press, 2008.

Spinks, David — *The Business of Belonging: How to Make Community Your Competitive Advantage.* Hoboken, NJ: Wiley, 2021.

Wertheim, Suzanne — *The Inclusive Language Field Guide: 6 Simple Principles for Avoiding Painful Mistakes and Communicating Respectfully.* Kindle Edition. (Year not provided).

PEER-REVIEWED JOURNAL ARTICLES

Bargh, John A., and Katelyn Y. A. McKenna. "The Internet and Social Life." *Annual Review of Psychology* 55 (2004): 573–590.

Ellison, Nicole B., Charles Steinfield, and Cliff Lampe. "The Benefits of Facebook 'Friends': Social Capital and College Students' Use of Online Social Network Sites." *Journal of Computer-Mediated Communication* 12, no. 4 (2007): 1143–1168.

Hampton, Keith N., and Barry Wellman. "Neighboring in Netville: How the Internet Supports Community in a Wired Suburb." *City & Community* 2, no. 4 (2003): 277–311.

Ridings, Catherine M., and David Gefen. "Virtual Community Attraction: Why People Hang Out Online." *Journal of Computer-Mediated Communication* 10, no. 1 (2004): Article 4.

Shaw, Lindsay H., and Larry M. Gant. "In Defense of the Internet: The Relationship Between Internet Communication and Depression, Loneliness, Self-Esteem, and Perceived Social Support." *CyberPsychology & Behavior* 5, no. 2 (2002): 157–171.

Steinkuehler, Constance, and Dmitri Williams. "Where Everybody Knows Your (Screen) Name: Online Games as 'Third Places.'" *Journal of Computer-Mediated Communication* 11, no. 4 (2006): 885–909.

Wellman, Barry, Anabel Quan-Haase, James Witte, and Keith Hampton. "Does the Internet Increase, Decrease, or Supplement Social Capital? Social Networks, Participation, and Community Commitment." *American Behavioral Scientist* 45, no. 3 (2001): 436–455.

ARTICLES, REPORTS, BUSINESS PUBLICATIONS, AND RESEARCH INSTITUTES

Armstrong, Arthur, and John Hagel III. "The Real Value of Online Communities." *Harvard Business Review* 74, no. 3 (1996): 134–141.

Bussgang, Jeffrey J., and Jono Bacon. "When Community Becomes Your Competitive Advantage." *Harvard Business Review* (digital article, January 21, 2020).

Hampton, Keith N., Lauren F. Sessions, Eun Ja Her, and Lee Rainie. Social Isolation and New Technology. *Pew Internet & American Life Project*, November 2009.

Horrigan, John B. "Online Communities." *Pew Internet & American Life Project*, October 31, 2001.

Williams, Ruth L., and Joseph Cothrel. "Four Smart Ways to Run Online Communities." *MIT Sloan Management Review* 41, no. 4 (Summer 2000): 81–91.

WEB RESOURCES

The Community Roundtable. *The State of Community Management* 2020. Research report, 2020.

Jamme, Lady Marieme, and Bhushan Sethi. "How Communities Can Become the Currency for Businesses to Build Skills." World Economic Forum, July 10, 2023.

Nielsen, Jakob. "Participation Inequality: Encouraging More Users to Contribute." Nielsen Norman Group (Alertbox), October 9, 2006.

PODCASTS

> **NOTE:** These podcasts and the videos that follow were accessible at the time of writing in March 2025.

Community Signal. Hosted by Patrick O'Keefe. Podcast series, 2015–present.

In Before the Lock. Hosted by Erica Kuhl and Brian Oblinger. Podcast series, 2019–present.

Masters of Community. Hosted by David Spinks. Podcast series, 2020–present.

YOUTUBE VIDEOS (EXPERT TALKS ON COMMUNITY FORMATION AND ENGAGEMENT)

Bacon, Jono. "The Future of Community." Talk at O'Reilly OSCON, July 2011. YouTube video, 29:30.

Godin, Seth. "The Tribes We Lead." TED Talk (TED2009), February 2009. Video, 17:33.

Turkle, Sherry. "Connected, but Alone?" TED Talk (TED2012), February 2012. Video, 19:48.

ABOUT THE AUTHOR

DR. EVE KEDAR

Dr. Eve Kedar doesn't just talk about transformation, she makes it happen. Known for her depth of knowledge, experience, and direct approach to sales enablement and community building, Eve has been the secret weapon behind performance breakthroughs at tech giants like Apple, Seagate, and Gainsight, as well as nimble startups and communities ready to scale.

Eve's first book, *Build a Kicka$$ Sales Team: Practical Sales Tactics,* is your go-to playbook for leaders tired of theoretical fluff and hungry for actionable strategies that work. Now she's bringing that same results-driven, inclusive approach to community building.

Here's the thing about Eve: She gets that vibrant communities aren't just nice-to-haves, they're **rocket fuel for organizations**. With her doctorate in Education and Leadership for Change from Fielding Graduate University, she approaches community building with an evidence-based methodology that creates spaces where people don't just connect, they thrive and transform together. Her global, inclusive approach ensures that communities under her guidance genuinely encompass diverse perspectives.

As a devoted practitioner of Loretta Ross's "calling in" approach, Eve builds communities where accountability comes with compassion and where people can learn, experiment, and grow in a trusted environment. Innovation happens in environments where people feel safe to take risks.

Eve's commitment to inclusive community building extends beyond the corporate world through her work with TIC—Thrive, Include, Connect—a community she's helping build to support parents of diverse learners. This passion project exemplifies her belief that well-designed communities are powerful forces for positive change and support in people's lives.

When she's not revolutionizing how organizations build and nurture communities, Eve lives with her wife and their two dogs in California. She also volunteers as a guide at the Monterey Bay Aquarium, where she brings the same passion for connection and education to curious visitors of all ages.

Whether you're looking to supercharge your sales team or build a community that becomes the envy of your industry, Dr. Eve Kedar is the expert you want in your corner. She doesn't just help you dream big; she gives you the tactical playbook to turn those dreams into reality. Connect with her on LinkedIn and discover how her kickass approach can transform your organization.